Chapter 1: Addition 1

Introducing the thousand

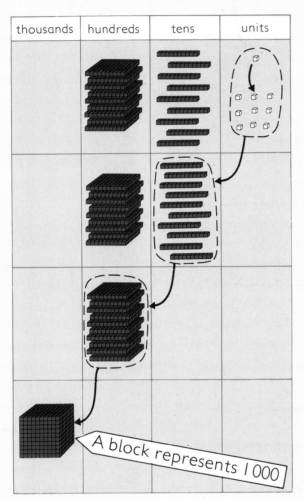

thousands	hundreds	tens	units

A block represents 1 000

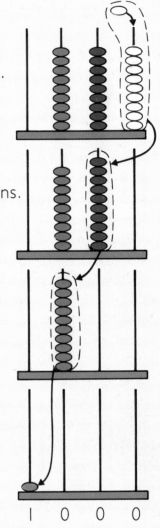

I is added to 999.

10 units
are exchanged
for I ten.

This makes 10 tens.

10 tens
are exchanged
for I hundred.

This makes
10 hundreds.

10 hundreds
are exchanged
for I <u>thousand</u>.

1   0   0   0

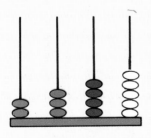

Two thousand
three hundred
and forty-five
looks like this:

2   3   4   5 → 5 (5 units)
→ 40 (4 tens)
→ 300 (3 hundreds)
→ 2000 (2 thousands)

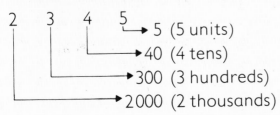

thousands	hundreds	tens	units

1 Here are some numbers set out in blocks, squares, longs and units or in tokens.
Draw an abacus picture and write each number in figures and in words.

a

thousands	hundreds	tens	units

b

thousands	hundreds	tens	units

c

thousands	hundreds	tens	units
thousand 1 000 thousand 1000	hundred 100	ten 10	

d

thousands	hundreds	tens	units
		ten 10	unit 1
thousand 1000		ten 10	unit 1
		ten 10	

2 Copy these abacus pictures. Write the number each shows in figures and in words.

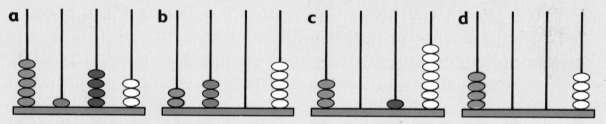

3 Draw abacus pictures for these and write the numbers in figures underneath.

   a Seven thousand two hundred and forty-eight.
   b Eight thousand seven hundred and eighteen.
   c One thousand and one.   **e** Six thousand and sixty.
   d Two thousand and twelve.   **f** Nineteen hundred and ninety.

4 Add 1 to each of these numbers. Draw an abacus picture of your answer and write it in words and figures.
   a 1094   **b** 2129   **c** 5039   **d** 3992   **e** 2099   **f** 999

5 Repeat question 4 but this time add 10 to each number.

Adding thousands, hundreds, tens and units

thousands	hundreds	tens	units

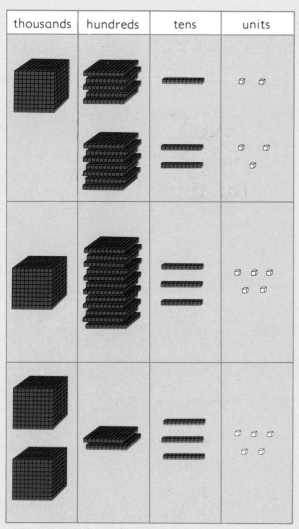

This is how the counting board is used to add 1512 and 723.

Set out 1512:

$$1000 + 500 + 10 + 2$$

and 723:

$$700 + 20 + 3$$

Add them together:

$$1000 + 1200 + 30 + 5$$

Exchange 10 hundred squares for 1 thousand block:

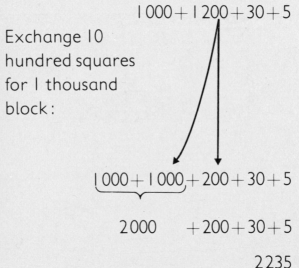

$$1000 + 1000 + 200 + 30 + 5$$

$$2000 \qquad + 200 + 30 + 5$$

$$2235$$

1 Use some blocks, squares, longs and units (or tokens)

thousand 1000	hundred 100	ten 10	unit 1

on a counting board for these:

a   1512
  + 340

c   736
  +2441

e   2176
  +2024

g   4783
  +1146

i   3927
  +4846

b   2653
  +1542

d   863
  + 844

f   3002
  +1139

h   1927
  +2073

j   345
  + 656

We can add 2372 and 1416 like this:

$$2372 \longrightarrow 2000+300+70+2$$
$$+1416 \longrightarrow 1000+400+10+6$$
$$3788 \longleftarrow 3000+700+80+8$$

1 Set these out the same way.

a 2174
  +3723

b   718
  +2131

c 1357
  +8642

d 5665
  +2024

$$1463 \longrightarrow 1000 \quad + \quad 400 \quad + \quad 60 \quad + \quad 3$$
$$+3819 \longrightarrow 3000 \quad + \quad 800 \quad + \quad 10 \quad + \quad 9$$
$$4000 \quad + \quad 1200 \quad + \quad 70 \quad + \quad 12$$
$$4000+1000+200 \quad + \quad 70+10 \quad + \quad 2$$
$$5282 \longleftarrow 5000 \quad +200 \quad + \quad 80 \quad + \quad 2$$

2 Set these out in the same way:

a 1575
  +2319

b 3424
  + 765

c 5386
  +1819

d 4388
  +1831

Horizontal layout

$$2378 \longrightarrow 2000+300+ 70+ 8$$
$$+4149 \longrightarrow 4000+100+ 40+ 9$$
$$6000+400+110+17$$
$$6527 \longleftarrow 6000+500+20+7$$

Vertical layout

  2378
+4149
   17   (8+9)
  110   (70+40)
  400   (300+100)
6000   (2000+4000)
6527

3 Set these out vertically.

a 1675
  +3279

b 4306
  +1274

c 3675
  + 895

d 1362
  +2028

e 1696
  +2604

Here is an even shorter way of recording addition.

$6+9 = 15 \rightarrow$ 1 ten and 5 units
Write 5 in the 'units' column of answer
and 1 below in 'tens' column

```
 2536
+4829
────
    5
────
  1
```

$30+20+10 = 60 \rightarrow$ 6 tens
Write 6 in the 'tens' column of answer.

```
 2536
+4829
────
   65
────
  1
```

$500+800 = 1300 \rightarrow$ 1 thousand and 3 hundreds
Write three in 'hundreds' column of answer and
1 below in 'thousands' column.

```
 2536
+4829
────
  365
────
 1  1
```

$2000+4000+1000 = 7000$
Write 7 in 'thousands' column.

```
 2536
+4829
────
 7365
────
 1  1
```

1 Use the shorter way of recording for these:

a	1465	**c**	5428	**e**	1978	**g**	72	**i**	69
	+2217		+1742		+2978		8		1701
							+619		+2150

b	3291	**d**	4536	**f**	1235	**h**	1037	**j**	1549
	+1476		+3464		312		337		2439
					+1251		+ 37		+3076

2  *Be sure to write figures in the correct columns.*

    a $7007+707+77$
    b $1732+6+109$
    c $39+762+440+14$
    d $2106+210+106+26$

6

1

Be sure to set figures in the correct columns. The first one is done for you.

a Add six thousand and six, six hundred and sixteen and sixty-six

```
  6006
   616
+   66
_____
```

b Add five thousand five hundred and five to five thousand and fifteen.

c Find the total of eight thousand and eighty-eight, eighteen and eight hundred and eight.

2 Write down the answers to:
a 1 more than 1999.　　**b** 200 less than 2000.
c 100 more than 1955.
d Find the total of your answers to **a**, **b** and **c**.

3 If a man is born in 1969 and lives for 75 years, in which year will he die?

4 Queen Victoria came to the throne in 1837 and reigned for 64 years, in which year did she die?

5 An odometer shows the number of kilometres a car has travelled.

a A man buys a car which shows 　4 3 7 6　 on the odometer. In one week he travels 828 kilometres; what does the odometer show now?

b In the second week, he travels another 1052 kilometres, what does the odometer show now?

c How many kilometres did he travel in the two weeks?

6 Add together:

a numbers in the circles
b numbers in the squares
c numbers in the triangles
d the odd numbers
e the even numbers

923　　2347　　1586

1024　　1705　　466

f Check that the sum of the answers **a**, **b** and **c** equals the sum of answers **d** and **e**.

Chapter 2: Shape 1

Angles-degree measurement

Using very simple instruments the Babylonians, before 4000 B.C., had the mistaken idea that the Sun travelled round the Earth and that it took only 360 days. Because of this they divided a complete turn into 360 parts and called each part
a degree (written as 1°).

One complete turn = 360°.
Half a complete turn = 180°.
A quarter of a complete turn or one right-angle = 90°.

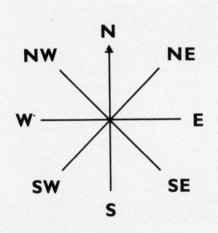

1 The angle between N and E measured in a clockwise direction is a right angle. How many degrees is it?

2 The angle between N and NE measured in a clockwise direction is half a right angle. How many degrees is it?

3 The angle between N and SW measured in an anti-clockwise direction is $1\frac{1}{2}$ right angles. How many degrees is it?

4 Copy and complete

I start facing	I turn through	Direction	I finish facing
North	180°	Clockwise	
South	90°	Anti-clockwise	
East	360°	Clockwise	
West	135°	Clockwise	
North East	225°		South
South West		Clockwise	South East
North West	270°		North East
South East		Clockwise	North
South East	315°		South
South East		Anti-clockwise	West

1 How many degrees does the minute hand of a clock turn through in one hour?

2 How long does it take the hour hand to turn through 360°?

3 How many degrees does the minute hand turn through in a quarter of an hour?

4 How many degrees does the minute hand turn through in 5 minutes?

5 In three hours the hour hand turns through how many degrees?

6 How many degrees does the hour hand turn through in one hour?

7 Copy and complete:

Hand of clock	From	To	Turns through (degrees)
hour hand	1	4	
minute hand	3	6	
minute hand	2	8	
hour hand	5	11	
minute hand	4	8	
hour hand	6	11	
minute hand	11	4	
hour hand	10	5	

Describing angles

A **right angle** = 90°

An **acute angle** is less than a right angle so an acute angle is less than 90°.

An **obtuse angle** is more than one right angle but less than two right angles so an obtuse angle is more than 90° but less than 180°.

8 List these angles and say whether they are acute or obtuse.

a 36° c 79° e 163° g 110° i 34° k 21°

b 141° d 88° f 17° h 96° j 175° l 169°

Angles of a triangle

1 Draw any triangle on
a piece of paper.
Mark the angles **A**, **B** and **C**
as in the diagram.

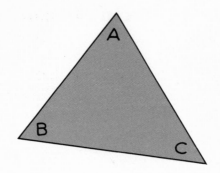

Tear off each angle as shown:

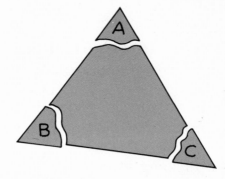

Stick the three angles in
your book like this:

Together they make 180° or
two right angles.

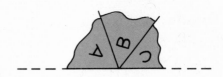

> The angles of a triangle add up to 180°.

2 For each triangle calculate the size of the unmarked angle:

a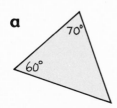

b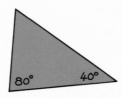

c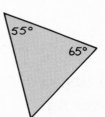

d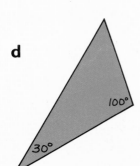

e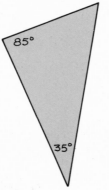

f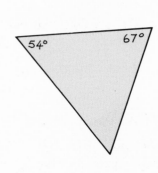

Angles in special triangles

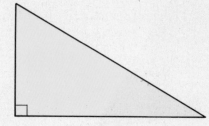

A triangle with one angle of 90° is called a **right-angled triangle.** The right angle is often marked as in the diagram.

A triangle with its three sides equal is called an **equilateral triangle**. It also has three equal angles.

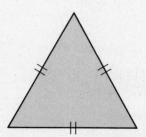

I How many degrees is each angle?

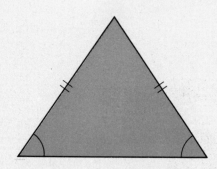

A triangle with two equal sides is an **isosceles triangle**. It has two equal angles.

2 If one of the equal angles of an isosceles triangle is 55°, what are the sizes of the other two angles in the triangle?

Draw a square and the diagonal shown in the diagram.

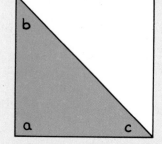

3 How many degrees is the angle marked **a**?

4 How many is the angle marked **b**?

5 How many is the angle marked **c**?

6 Describe the triangle shaded in the diagram in two different ways.

7 For each triangle, calculate the size of the angles marked with letters.

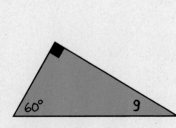
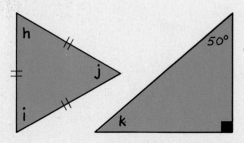
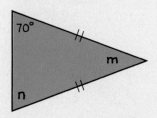

Chapter 3: Subtraction 1

Splitting thousands

A **block** represents 1000.  It can be exchanged for 10 **squares** (ten hundreds)

1 thousand token  is worth 10 hundred tokens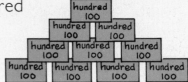

For 3245 − 1419
Set out 3245 as
3(1000)+2(100)+4(10)+5(1).

There are not enough units and not enough hundreds to take away.
1(1000)+4(100)+1(10) + 9(1).

Exchange a 1000 block for ten 100 squares and a 10 rod for ten units, so that there are
2(1000)+12(100)+3(10)+15(1)

thousands	hundreds	tens	units

thousands	hundreds	tens	units

Now you can take away 1419 leaving the answer: 1826.

Record like this:

```
3245    ⟶    (3000 + 200 + 40 + 5)  ⟶   (2000 + 1200 + 30 + 15)
−1419   ⟶   −(1000 + 400 + 10 + 9)  ⟶  −(1000 +  400 + 10 +  9)
─────                                     ──────────────────────
1826    ⟵─────────────────────────────   (1000 +  800 + 20 +  6)
```

1 Use blocks, squares, longs and units or token cards for these :
   a 2174 − 851 **b** 3561 − 1825 **c** 1632 − 856 **d** 4000 − 2345

2 Copy and complete to show the exchange in question **d**.
   4000 = ☐ (1000) + ☐ (100) + ☐ (10) + ☐ (1)

This is how 3245 − 1419 is set out the short way :

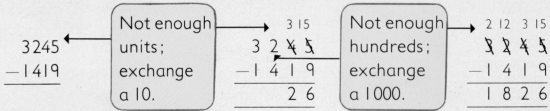

$$\begin{array}{r} 3245 \\ -1419 \\ \hline \end{array}$$ → Not enough units; exchange a 10. → $$\begin{array}{r} {}^{3\ 15} \\ 3\ 2\ \cancel{4}\ \cancel{5} \\ -1\ 4\ 1\ 9 \\ \hline 2\ 6 \end{array}$$ → Not enough hundreds; exchange a 1000. → $$\begin{array}{r} {}^{2\ 12\ 3\ 15} \\ \cancel{3}\ \cancel{2}\ \cancel{4}\ \cancel{5} \\ -1\ 4\ 1\ 9 \\ \hline 1\ 8\ 2\ 6 \end{array}$$

$\overset{2\ 12\ 3\ 15}{\cancel{3}\ \cancel{2}\ \cancel{4}\ \cancel{5}}$ shows that 3(1000) + 2(100) + 4(10) + 5(1)
were exchanged for 2(1000) + 12(100) + 3(10) + 15(1)

3 Try these. Some have been started for you.

a $$\begin{array}{r} {}^{1\ 13} \\ \cancel{2}\ \cancel{3}\ 4\ 0 \\ -1\ 8\ 2\ 0 \\ \hline \end{array}$$ **c** $$\begin{array}{r} {}^{9\ 14\ 10} \\ \cancel{1}\ \cancel{0}\ \cancel{5}\ \cancel{0} \\ -\ \ 9\ 7\ 9 \\ \hline \end{array}$$ **e** $$\begin{array}{r} 5000 \\ -2345 \\ \hline \end{array}$$ **g** $$\begin{array}{r} 3372 \\ -1493 \\ \hline \end{array}$$ **i** $$\begin{array}{r} 4321 \\ -1234 \\ \hline \end{array}$$

b $$\begin{array}{r} {}^{7\ 11\ 15} \\ 4\ \cancel{8}\ \cancel{2}\ \cancel{5} \\ -2\ 5\ 3\ 7 \\ \hline \end{array}$$ **d** $$\begin{array}{r} {}^{7\ 9\ 9\ 10} \\ \cancel{8}\ \cancel{0}\ \cancel{0}\ \cancel{0} \\ -6\ 0\ 5\ 2 \\ \hline \end{array}$$ **f** $$\begin{array}{r} 4225 \\ -2537 \\ \hline \end{array}$$ **h** $$\begin{array}{r} 7120 \\ -2389 \\ \hline \end{array}$$ **j** $$\begin{array}{r} 5104 \\ -3826 \\ \hline \end{array}$$

4 The graph shows the points scored by four teams.

Green team's score	1225
Red team's score	− 950
Difference	275

Find the difference between the scores of :
   a The Blue and Yellow teams
   b The Yellow and Red teams
   c The Green and Yellow teams
   d The Green and Blue teams

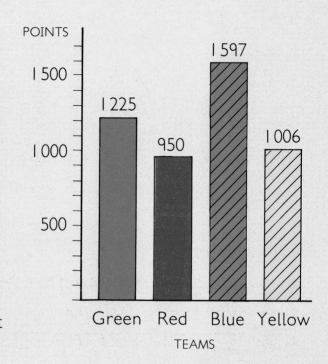

5 How much greater is the highest than the lowest score?

How many points must Red win to equal Green's score?
The question is asking:

950 and how many make 1 225?

or $950 + \square = 1\,225$

To find the **difference** between 950 and 1 225 we can
either subtract   or add
$1\,225 - 950 = \square$ $950 + \square = 1\,225$

Difference problems can be
solved by 'making up' the
smaller to the larger number
using a zig-zag layout.

For example, $1\,518 + \boxed{1\,627} = 3\,145$

or $3\,145 - 1\,518 = \boxed{1\,627}$

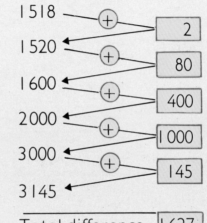

Total difference $\boxed{1\,627}$

1   Rewrite each sentence as an addition problem, then use the zig-zag
layout to find the difference. The first one is done for you.

a $167 - 128 = \square$ c $2\,035 - 1\,679 = \square$ e $6\,371 - 4\,298 = \square$
b $1\,410 - 1\,286 = \square$ d $4\,203 - 2\,345 = \square$ f $8\,009 - 5\,290 = \square$

a $128 + \boxed{} = 167$

$128 + \boxed{39} = 167$

or $167 - 128 = 39$

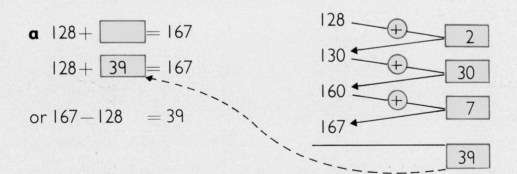

2   Try doing these 'in your head' using the 'making up' method.
Write down the answers and then check by a written method.

a $28 + \square = 60$ c $790 + \square = 1\,000$ e $1\,784 + \square = 2\,000$
b $86 + \square = 131$ d $168 + \square = 501$ f $1\,890 + \square = 3\,224$

1 Work out numbers to go in the empty frames lettered **a**, **b**, **c**, **d**, **e**, **f** and **g**.

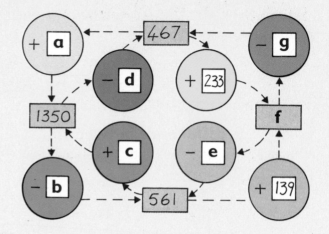

2 So far Anne has read 768 pages of a book with 1 025 pages in it. How many more pages must she read to finish the book?

3 How much greater is the capacity of a Cortina (1 593 cm³) than a Mini (998 cm³)?

4 Station

J

Bus stop

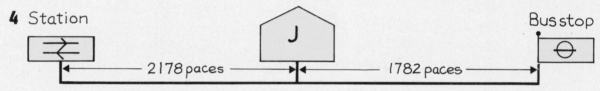

2178 paces   1782 paces

John paces the distances from his house to the station and, in the opposite direction, to the bus stop.

  a How much farther is the station than the bus stop from his house?

  b How many paces is it from the station to the bus stop?

5 Here are the dates of some Royal families who have ruled England.

Normans	1066 to 1154
Plantagenets	1154 to 1485
Tudors	1485 to 1603
House of Hanover	1714 to 1901

  a Which family ruled the longest?

  b Which family ruled the shortest time?

  c How many more years did the Plantagenets rule than the Tudors?

  d How many years shorter was Norman rule than the House of Hanover's rule?

6 At the start of a journey the odometer shows 7 7 8 6 km and 8 0 2 5 km at the end. How long was the journey?

7 What is the difference in price of a car costing £6 582 and a caravan costing £3 825.

Chapter 4: Area 1

Areas and perimeters

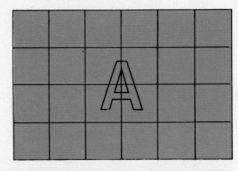

Use a ruler to copy these rectangles on to squared centimetre paper.

Rectangle A has 6 cm² in a row and 4 rows.
$6 \times 4 = 24$
so area of A = 24 cm²

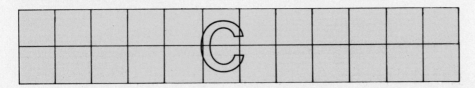

1 Copy the table and fill in the first 3 columns.

	Length in centimetres	Breadth in centimetres	Area in square centimetres	Perimeter in centimetres
A	6cm	4cm	24cm²	. . . . .cm
B				
C				

Perimeter is the distance around a shape.
Do you remember a quick way to work out the perimeters of rectangles?
Fill in the 4th column of your table.

2 Write a sentence about the areas and perimeters of **A**, **B** and **C**.

3 Draw these on cm-squared paper and answer the questions.
   a Rectangle **D** is 7cm long, 3cm wide. Find its area and perimeter.
   b Rectangle **E** is 9cm long, 1cm wide. Find its area and perimeter.
   c The area of rectangle **F** is 16cm² and it is 8cm long.
     Find its breadth and perimeter.
   d Square **G** has a perimeter of 20cm. Find its area.

4 Write a sentence about the areas and perimeters of **D**, **E**, **F** and **G**.

Making shapes

Cut out a square 10cm by 10cm
from card.

Mark and cut out the 5 shapes:
1 rectangle and 4 equal triangles.
(The diagrams are half size.)

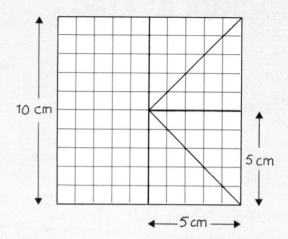

10 cm

5 cm

←—5 cm—→

1   Use all five pieces
    without overlapping
    to make each shape
    and copy it onto
    1cm² paper.

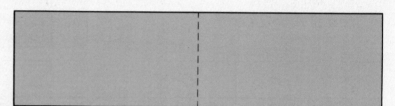

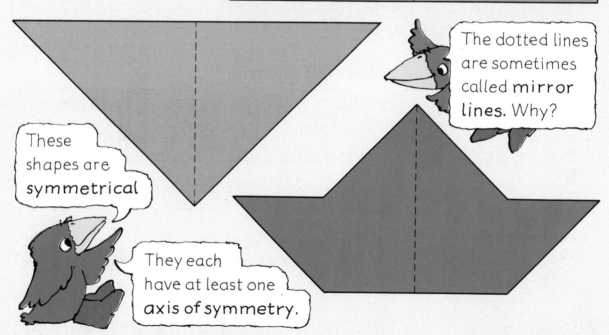

The dotted lines
are sometimes
called **mirror
lines**. Why?

These
shapes are
symmetrical

They each
have at least one
axis of symmetry.

2   a What is the area of each shape in question 1?
    b Measure and record the perimeter of each shape.
    c Write a sentence about the area and perimeters.

3   Make some more shapes with the 5 pieces.
    Record them on 1cm² squared paper.
    Mark in any axes of symmetry.
    Measure and record the perimeters.

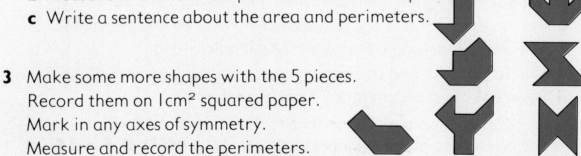

Larger areas

On cm² paper draw a square with sides 10cm long.

Carefully cut out the square—you will need it later.

Copy the sentence about the area on to your square.

10 cm

The area of this square
is 100 square centimetres

or

1 square decimetre
$100 \text{ cm}^2 = 1 \text{ dm}^2$

←————— 10cm —————→

I Estimate how many of your squares would be needed to cover:
 a your desk top   **c** a flagstone in the playground
 b the classroom door **d** a classroom window pane

The best way to estimate is to try to imagine how many of your squares would fit into a row and how many rows.

For example: 8 in a row; 4 rows
$8 \times 4 = 32$

Estimate 32dm²
   or 3200cm²

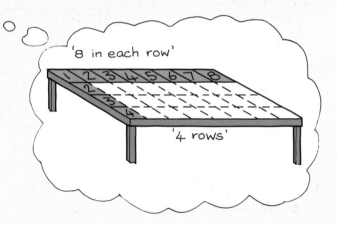

'8 in each row'

'4 rows'

2 Use your square cut-out to check how accurate your estimates were for question **I**.
 Record the areas **a** in square decimetres (dm²) and
            b in square centimetres (cm²).

The diagrams of two table tops had to be drawn smaller than they really are in order to fit them on this page.

They are drawn to **scale**.

1cm represents 10cm (or 1dm)
1cm² represents 100cm² (or 1dm²)

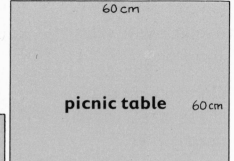

picnic table 60 cm

100 cm

coffee table 30 cm

1 a How many of your 1dm² squares are needed to cover each table?
   b What is the area of each table in cm²?
   c Which table has the greater area and by how many cm²?
   d What is the perimeter of each table in cm?
   e Write a sentence about the areas
      and perimeters of the tables.

2 Copy each shape on 1cm² paper
   using the **scale**.
   1cm represents 10cm (1dm)
   1cm² represents 100cm² (1dm²)

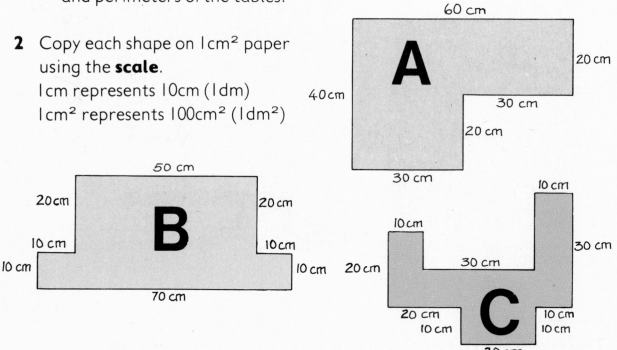

Copy and complete this table.

Shape	Number of dm² to cover	Area in cm²	Perimeter in cm
A			
B			
C			

1 Make a square metre by using a metre rule and sheets of newspaper; or using 4 metre rules; or pegging out string. (How long will the string be?)

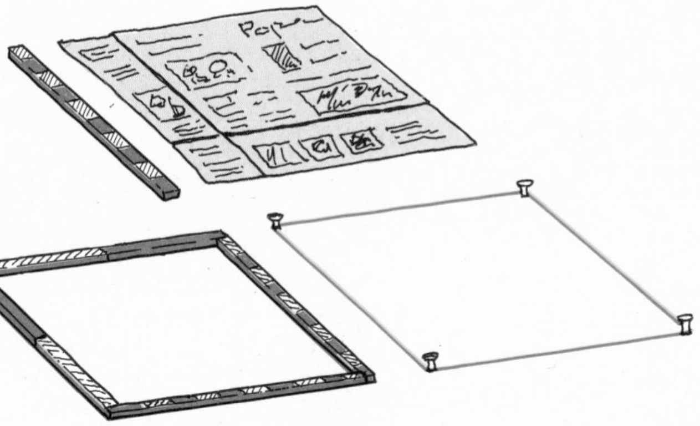

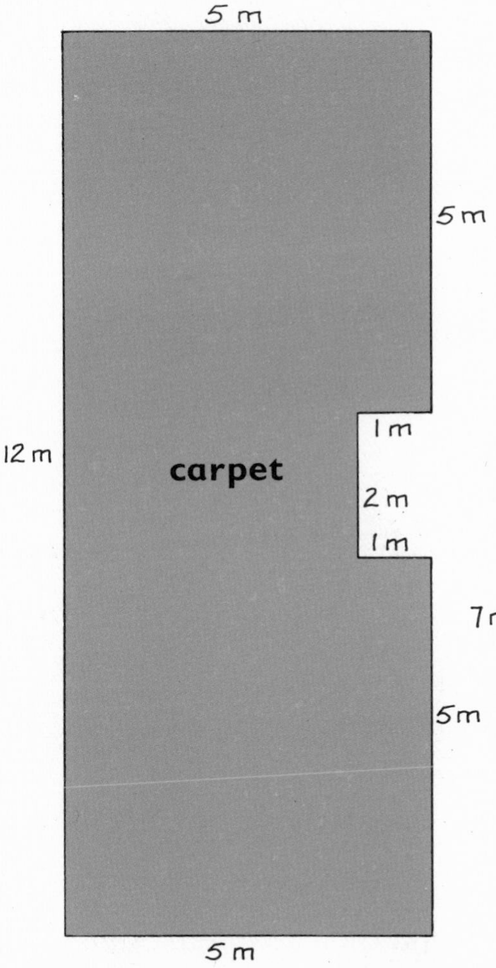

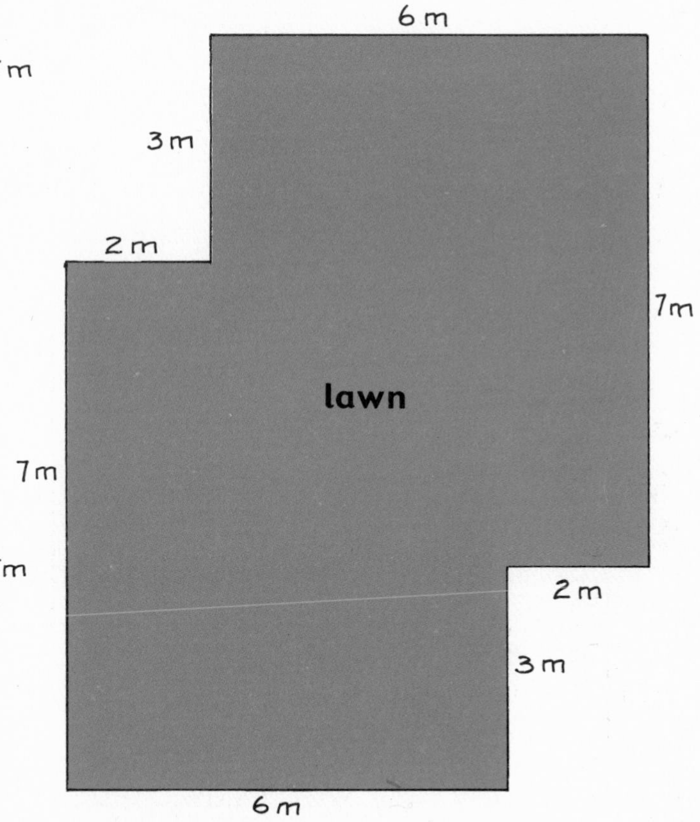

5 m

5 m

12 m

carpet

1 m

2 m

1 m

7 m

5 m

5 m

6 m

3 m

2 m

7 m

lawn

2 m

3 m

6 m

2 a Find the area and perimeter of the carpet and of the lawn. Write a sentence about your results.
   b What is the cost of the carpet at £8 per m²?
   c If it takes 5 minutes to mow 10m², could you mow the lawn in under half an hour?
   d How long will it take to trim the edge (perimeter) of the lawn if you can trim 2 metres in a minute?

Chapter 5: Multiplication 1

This diagram shows 17×6.   It is set out like this:

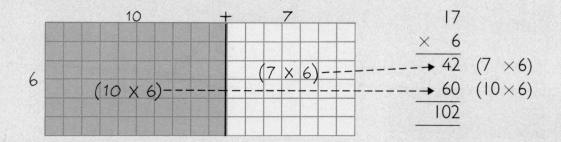

1 Do these the same way:

a	13	**b**	16	**c**	18	**d**	17	**e**	19
	× 4		× 7		× 6		× 9		× 8

For larger numbers we can use paper with smaller squares.
This diagram shows 23×8.   It is set out like this:

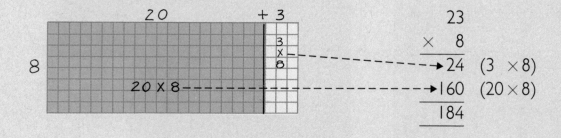

2 Do these in the same way. Draw a diagram and then set them out.

a	24	**c**	28	**e**	34	**g**	57	**i**	59
	× 3		× 6		× 8		× 5		× 7
b	31	**d**	37	**f**	46	**h**	48	**j**	47
	× 4		× 7		× 9		× 8		× 6

3 Set these out and complete them without using a diagram.

a	43	**b**	37	**c**	63	**d**	54	**e**	76
	× 6		× 8		× 7		× 9		× 5

Flow charts

Multiplication can be set out like this:

27×7

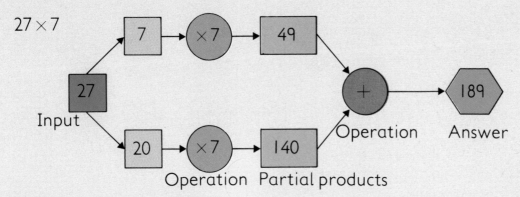

Here is another example

36×9

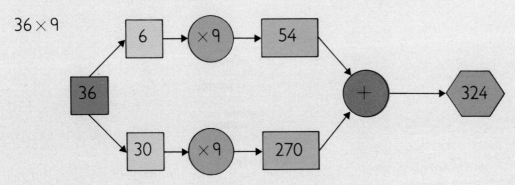

1 Copy and complete these diagrams

a 58×5

b 75×9

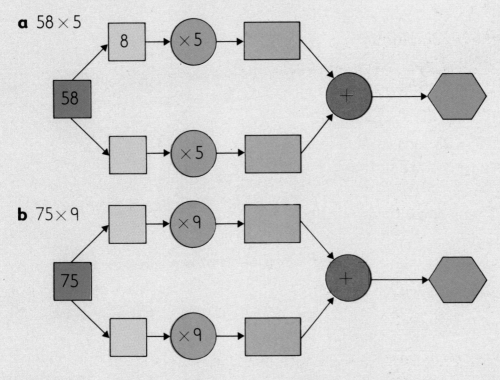

2 Do these in the same way, drawing your own diagram for each.
   a 73×6 **b** 89×8 **c** 96×7 **d** 68×8

A shorter way to multiply

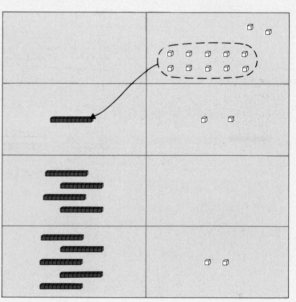

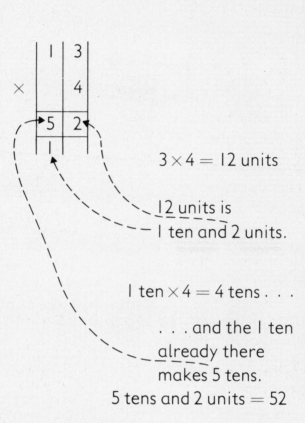

$3 \times 4 = 12$ units

12 units is
1 ten and 2 units.

1 ten $\times 4 = 4$ tens . . .

. . . and the 1 ten
already there
makes 5 tens.
5 tens and 2 units $= 52$

Here is another example: 34×7
$4 \times 7 = 28$
that is 2 tens and 8 units.

3 tens $\times 7 = 21$ tens. . .
. . . and the 2 tens already there
makes 23 tens.
2 hundreds 3 tens and 8 units $= 238$.

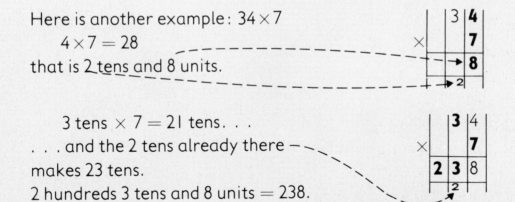

I Do these the same way

a	27	**c**	38	**e**	37	**g**	63	**i**	83
	× 3		× 5		× 4		× 8		× 7
b	34	**d**	43	**f**	57	**h**	49	**j**	92
	× 6		× 6		× 7		× 6		× 9

Multiplying hundreds, tens and units

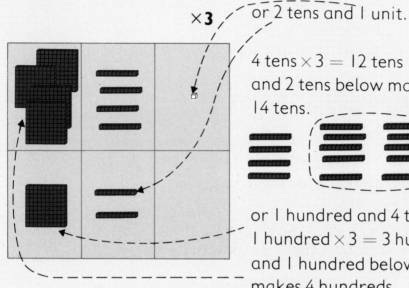

hundreds	tens	units

7 units × 3 = 21 units

or 2 tens and 1 unit.

4 tens × 3 = 12 tens
and 2 tens below make
14 tens.

or 1 hundred and 4 tens
1 hundred × 3 = 3 hundreds
and 1 hundred below
makes 4 hundreds.

Here is another example: 264 × 6

4 units × 6 = 24 units
that is, 2 tens and 4 units.
6 tens × 6 = 36 tens . . .
. . and the 2 tens below make
38 tens or 3 hundreds and 8 tens
2 hundreds × 6 = 12 hundreds . . .
. . and the 3 hundreds below make
15 hundreds or 1 thousand 5 hundreds.

1 Do these the same way:

a	134	c	176	e	645	g	483
	× 3		× 4		× 8		× 7

b	225	d	328	f	396	h	627
	× 5		× 6		× 9		× 9

1 a If there are 16 crayons in a packet, how many will there be in 7 packets?

b How many buttons will be needed for 9 coats if each coat has 14 buttons on it?

c How much will 18 packets of crisps cost if each costs 8p?

d A packet contains 15 biscuits.
How many biscuits will there be in 6 packets?

e If my newspaper has 24 pages, how many pages will there be in 6 newspapers?

f A coach has seats for 37 children.
How many children can travel in 8 coaches?

g A carton holds two dozen boxes of soap.
How many boxes of soap will there be in 9 cartons.

h Lamp posts are placed 75 metres apart along a main road.
How far is it from the first lamp to the ninth lamp?
Warning—look at the diagram.

i There are 36 desks in each classroom of a school which has 9 classrooms. How many desks are there altogether?

j A bag of sweets costs 16p. How much will 15 bags cost?
(Give your answer first in pence then in £s.)

k If a ribbon is 18cm long, how far will 17 ribbons reach if they are put end to end?

l If there are 16 rows of tiles in the hall and each row has 18 tiles in it, how many tiles are there altogether?

m A bottle of perfume holds 18 millilitres.
How much perfume will 14 bottles contain?

Chapter 6 : Volume and Capacity

A **prism** can be thought of as a solid shape which could be cut into 'slices' or layers, all the same shape and size.

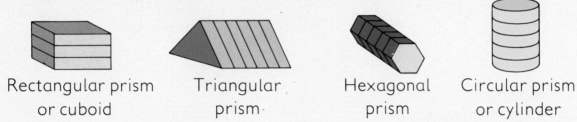

| Rectangular prism or cuboid | Triangular prism | Hexagonal prism | Circular prism or cylinder |

I Which of these shapes are prisms? Make a list, name and draw the shape of each 'slice' or layer like this :

Prism	Shape of 'slice'
B	square ☐

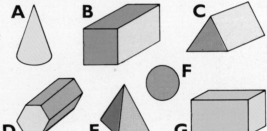

2 The **volume** of a prism is the amount of space it takes up. Find the volumes of these rectangular prisms by counting how many cubic centimetres (cm³) are used to make each one :

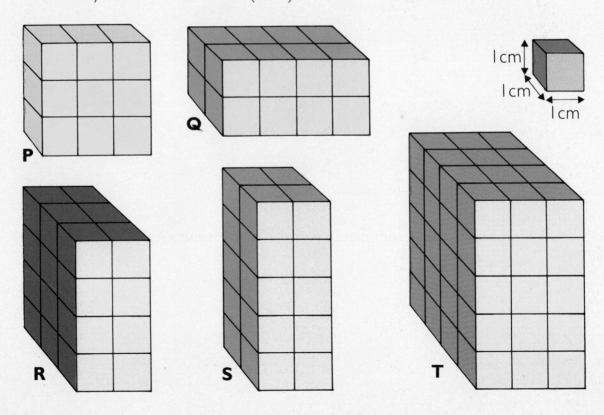

There is a quicker way to work
out the volume of a cuboid.

This cuboid looks like a sliced
loaf. It has 5 slices or
layers each 1cm thick.

The end slice contains
3 rows of 4 cubes,
that is 12cm³.

There are 5 slices or layers
with 12cm³ in each so
the volume is 12cm³ × 5 = 60cm³

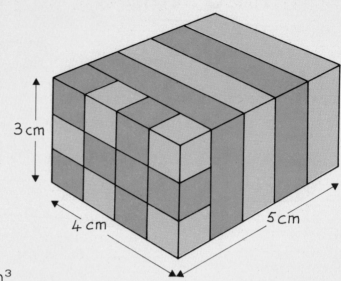

Volume of cuboid = | Number of cm³ in one layer | × | Number of layers |

1 Use centimetre cubes to make and find the volume of each
of these cuboids:

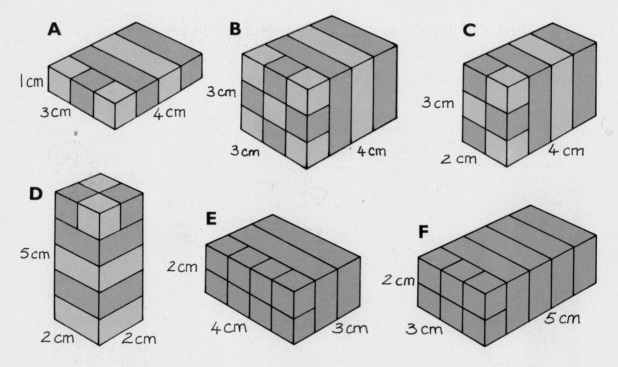

2 What do you notice about cuboids **C** and **E**?
Find other ways of making cuboids with the same volumes
as **A**, **B**, **D** and **F**.
In each case record how many cm³ in one layer and how many layers.

If we know the lengths of the edges of a cuboid we can find its volume without counting any cubes at all.

The area of the front face (the 'slice area') is 6 square centimetres.
Multiply this by the length to find the volume.

$$6cm^2 \times 4cm = 24cm^3$$

The correct name for the 'slice area' is the **area of cross-section**.
So the volume of a cuboid = area of cross section × length.

I Copy and complete the table for the volume of these cuboids.

Cuboid letter	Area of cross-section	Length	Volume
A	. . . . . . cm²	. . . cm	. . . cm³
B			

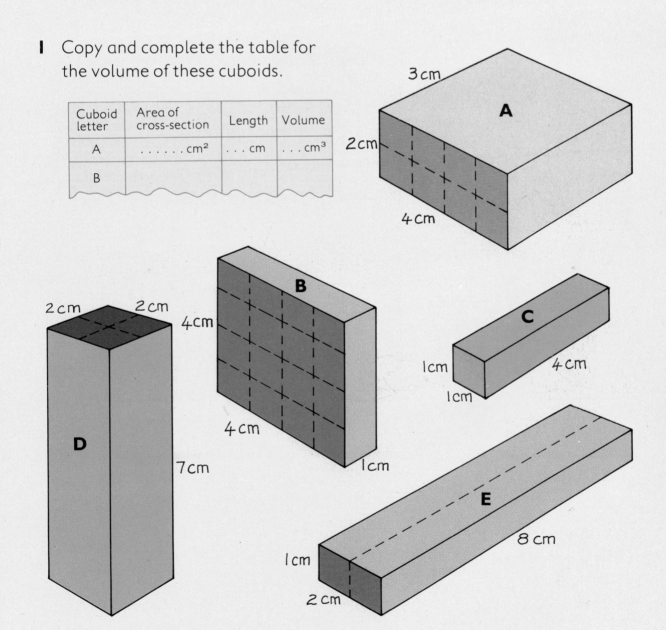

Volume = area of cross section × length   works for all prisms.

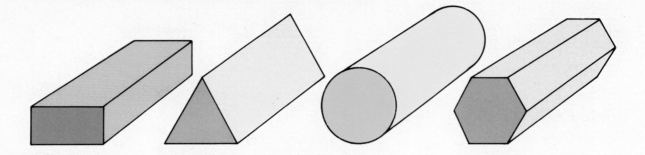

The area of cross-section of each of these prisms is 2cm² and each is 3cm long. The volume of each prism is 2cm² × 3cm = 6cm³.

1 Work out the volume of these prisms. The area of cross-section is shown on the end face.

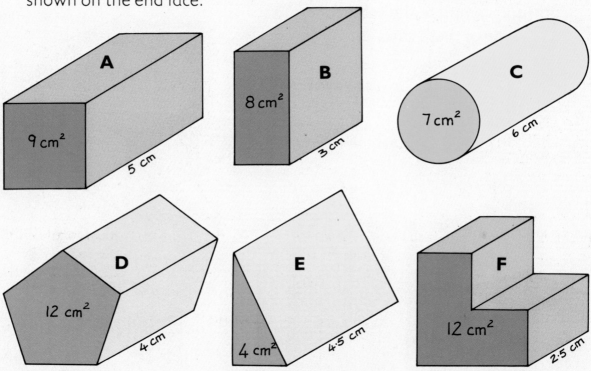

A 9 cm² 5 cm

B 8 cm² 3 cm

C 7 cm² 6 cm

D 12 cm² 4 cm

E 4 cm² 4·5 cm

F 12 cm² 2·5 cm

2 Copy and complete this table:

Area of end face square units	Length of prism length units	Volume of prism cubic units
15cm²	6cm	. . . . .cm³
22cm²	9cm	. . . . .cm³
100cm²	. . . . cm	1000cm³
. . . . .cm²	9cm	108cm³
6cm²	1·50m	. . . . .cm³

1 For each prism, first find the area of cross-section (shaded) in cm² then work out the volume in cm³.

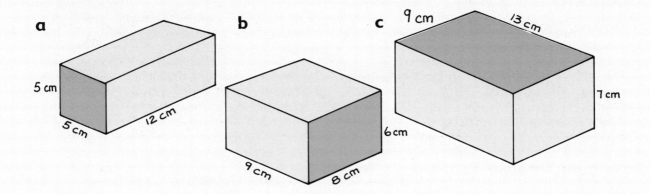

a 5 cm, 5 cm, 12 cm

b 9 cm, 6 cm, 8 cm

c 9 cm, 13 cm, 7 cm

The amount of space **inside** a hollow container is called its **internal volume** or **capacity**.
The capacity of a container is how much it will hold.
Many containers are shaped like prisms:

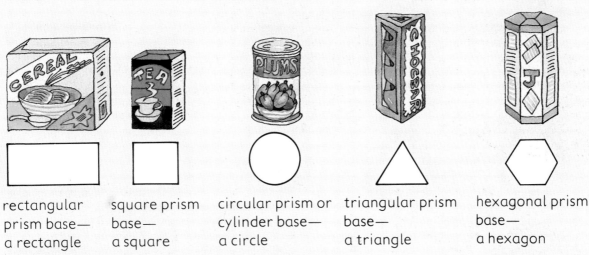

rectangular prism base— a rectangle

square prism base— a square

circular prism or cylinder base— a circle

triangular prism base— a triangle

hexagonal prism base— a hexagon

If the base of a prism is its cross-section, then the internal volume or capacity = base area × height.

2 Make a collection of containers and sort them out into those that are prisms and those that are not prisms.

3 Try to work out a way to find the approximate internal volume or capacity of a container which is a prism without opening it.

If a container is made from **thin** cardboard or metal, its **approximate capacity** can be worked out from outside measurements.

For some prisms you may have to find the area of cross-section by drawing round the base on centimetre-squared paper and counting the squares.

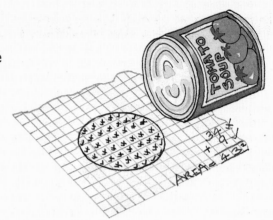

Whole squares (✗)   34
Half or more (✓)   + 9
Area $\simeq$ 43cm²

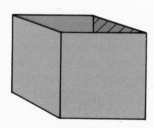

This hollow decimetre cube has a capacity of 1000cm³ or 1 litre.
Liquids are usually measured in litres or millilitres.
1000ml = 1 litre.
1ml of liquid takes up 1cm³ of space.

1   What is the base area of this fish tank in cm²?

2   What is the fish tank's capacity
     a in cm³?
     b in litres?

3   If the water in the tank is 11cm deep, what is the volume of water
     a in cm³?   **b** in litres?

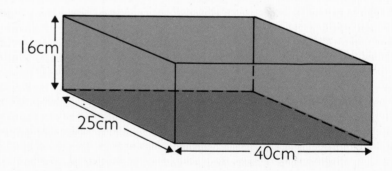

4   If another 2 litres of water is poured in, what will the new depth be?

5   Work out the measurements for other hollow cuboids which hold 1 litre, for example, 4cm × 10cm × 25cm.

Chapter 7: Division 1

In *Pupils' Book 4* you did some division questions like this:

```
        14 r 1
  4 ) 57
     -40 | 10 (4)
       17
     -16 |  4 (4)
        1 | 14 (4)
```

1 Do these the same way:

   a 73 ÷ 5   **c** 41 ÷ 3   **e** 68 ÷ 6   **g** 75 ÷ 6

   b 81 ÷ 7   **d** 93 ÷ 8   **f** 53 ÷ 4   **h** 93 ÷ 7

Look at this example: 3) 73

```
3 ) 73
 -30 | 10 (3)
   43 |
```

When 10 lots of 3 are subtracted there are so many left that 10 more lots of 3 can be taken away.

```
3 ) 73
 -30 | 10 (3)
   43 |
 -30 | 10 (3)
   13 |
```

Now four lots of 3 can be subtracted.

```
        24 r 1
3 ) 73
 -30 | 10 (3)
   43
 -30 | 10 (3)
   13
 -12 |  4 (3)
    1 | 24 (3)
```

2 Copy and complete these:

a
```
       □ r □
4 ) 95
 -40 | □ (4)
   55
 -□  | 10 (4)
   □
 -12 | □ (4)
    3 | □ (4)
```

b
```
        □ r □
2 ) 57
 -□  | 10 (2)
   □
 -□  | 10 (2)
   17
 -□  | □ (2)
   □ | □ (2)
```

c
```
        □ r □
3 ) 68
 -30 | □ (3)
   □
 -□  | □ (3)
   □
 -□  | □ (3)
   □ | □ (3)
```

Division of three digit numbers

$346 \div 9$
If the number to be divided is larger, we use the same method but we may need to subtract more lots of 10.

```
        38 r 4
9 ) 346
  -  90 | 10 (9)
     256
  -  90 | 10 (9)
     166
  -  90 | 10 (9)
      76
  -  72 |  8 (9)
       4 | 38 (9)
```

I Copy and complete these:

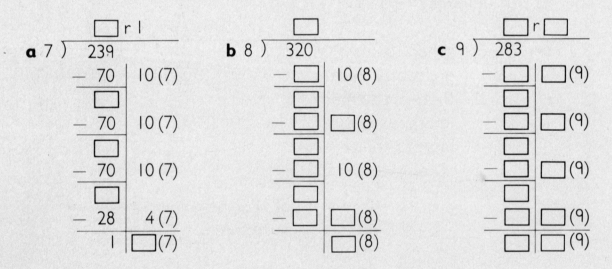

```
          □ r 1
a 7 ) 239
   -  70 | 10 (7)
      □
   -  70 | 10 (7)
      □
   -  70 | 10 (7)
      □
   -  28 |  4 (7)
       1 | □ (7)
```

```
          □
b 8 ) 320
   -  □ | 10 (8)
      □
   -  □ | □ (8)
      □
   -  □ | 10 (8)
      □
   -  □ | □ (8)
        | □ (8)
```

```
          □ r □
c 9 ) 283
   -  □ | □ (9)
      □
   -  □ | □ (9)
      □
   -  □ | □ (9)
      □
   -  □ | □ (9)
        | □ (9)
```

2 Do these, setting them out in the same way:

a $127 \div 4$ c $120 \div 3$ e $192 \div 6$ g $273 \div 7$

b $193 \div 5$ d $229 \div 7$ f $259 \div 8$ h $345 \div 9$

i 204 eggs are to be packed into boxes of 6.
How many boxes are needed?

j How many weeks are there in 252 days?

Shorter layout

Multiplication by 10 is quite simple. The digits move one column to the left and the units space is filled with a zero.

$$7 \times 10 = 70$$

$$27 \times 10 = 270$$

1 Copy and complete these:

a $9 \times 10 =$ **c** $14 \times 10 =$ **e** $23 \times 10 =$ **g** $48 \times 10 =$

b $11 \times 10 =$ **d** $19 \times 10 =$ **f** $34 \times 10 =$ **h** $73 \times 10 =$

Multiplication by a multiple of 10 (20, 30, 40, 50 . . .) is done in two steps like this:

$$7 \times 30 = 7 \times 3 \times 10 \qquad \longleftarrow \text{1st step}$$
$$= 21 \times 10$$
$$\qquad \longleftarrow \text{2nd step}$$
$$= \underline{\underline{210}}$$

$$56 \times 40 = 56 \times 4 \times 10 \qquad \longleftarrow \text{1st step}$$
$$= 224 \times 10$$
$$\qquad \longleftarrow \text{2nd step}$$
$$= \underline{\underline{2240}}$$

2 Copy and complete these:

a $9 \times 20 =$ **c** $12 \times 60 =$ **e** $34 \times 30 =$ **g** $68 \times 70 =$

b $8 \times 40 =$ **d** $27 \times 50 =$ **f** $53 \times 80 =$ **h** $79 \times 90 =$

Here is a shorter method for division:

```
        36 r 3
9 ) 327
   −270 | 30 (9)
     57
   − 54 |  6 (9)
      3 | 36 (9)
```

If we don't subtract all the lots of 10 together it doesn't matter. The longer way still works.

```
        36 r 3
9 ) 327
   −180 | 20 (9)
    147
   − 90 | 10 (9)
     57
   − 54 |  6 (9)
      3 | 36 (9)
```

1 Copy and complete these:

a 8) 346
   −320 | ☐ (8)
   ☐
   −☐ | ☐ (8)
   ☐ | ☐ (8)

   ☐ r ☐

b 7) 357
   −☐ | 50 (7)
   ☐
   −☐ | ☐ (7)
   ☐ | ☐ (7)

   ☐

c 9) 645
   −630 | ☐ (9)
   ☐
   ☐ | ☐ (9)
   ☐ | ☐ (9)

   ☐ r ☐

d 517 ÷ 6   f 434 ÷ 7   h 435 ÷ 5   j 647 ÷ 8   l 554 ÷ 6
e 223 ÷ 5   g 516 ÷ 8   i 522 ÷ 9   k 826 ÷ 9   m 365 ÷ 7

2 a In a forest 294 trees are planted in 7 rows.
   How many are in each row?

b If £448 is shared equally among 8 boys
   how much will each receive?

c There are 485 car tyres in a warehouse.
   How many cars would they provide tyres for?
   (Don't forget the spare wheel.)

d The perimeter of a regular octagon is 344cm.
   How long is one side?

e How many 5 millilitre spoonfuls of medicine can be poured
   from a bottle holding 285ml?

f A machine makes a toy every 8 minutes.
   How many does it make in 2 hours?

g How many egg boxes, each holding 6 eggs, will be needed
   to pack 504 eggs?

h A ribbon 9cm wide has an area of 162cm².
   How long is it?

i How many pens costing 8p each can you buy for £1.84?

j How many marbles, each weighing 7 grams, will weigh 168 grams?

Chapter 8: Length 1

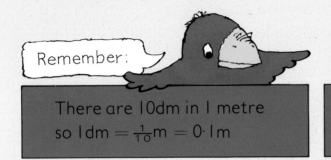

Remember:

| There are 10dm in 1 metre so $1dm = \frac{1}{10}m = 0.1m$ | There are 100cm in 1m so $1cm = \frac{1}{100}m = 0.01m$ |

The perimeter of this shape is 163cm. Add the lengths of the sides to check that this is correct.

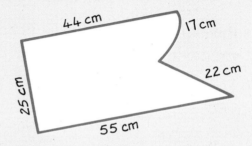

$$163cm = 100cm + 60cm + 3cm$$
$$= 1m + 6dm + 3cm$$
$$= 1m + \frac{6}{10}m + \frac{3}{100}m$$
$$= 1.00m + 0.60m + 0.03m$$
$$= 1.63m$$

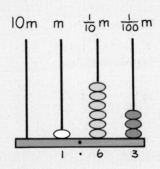

The abacus picture shows 1·63 metres.

1 Find the perimeters of these shapes in metres.
Record your answers in the same way with an abacus picture.

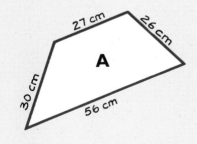

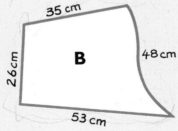

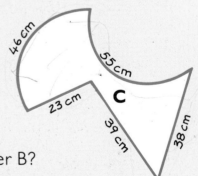

2 How much longer is perimeter C than perimeter B?

3 What is the difference between the perimeters of B and A?

4 The perimeter of a triangle is 1·25m. Two of the sides are 38cm and 45cm. Find the length of the third side.

Multiplication of metres and centimetres

An **equilateral** triangle has all its sides the same length.
To find the perimeter we can multiply the length of one side by 3.

Estimate first:

39cm ≃ 40cm,
so perimeter ≃ 120cm
            or 1·20m

Is the estimate
a good one? ⟵

$$\begin{array}{r} 39 \\ \times\quad 3 \\ \hline 27\ (9cm \times 3) \\ 90\ (30cm \times 3) \\ \hline 117cm\ or\ 1·17m \end{array}$$

39cm
39cm
39cm

I Use the same method of recording to find the perimeters of equilateral triangles with sides of **a** 54cm, **b** 83cm, **c** 67cm. Estimate each answer first.

2 A **polygon** is a flat shape with many corners and sides ('poly' means 'many' and 'gon' means 'corner').
Find some more words beginning with 'poly-' meaning 'many'.

3 A **regular** polygon has equal sides and equal angles.
Use multiplication to find the perimeters of these polygons in metres.
Remember to **estimate** first.

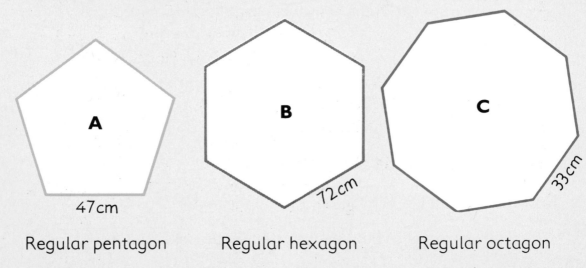

A
47cm
Regular pentagon

B
72cm
Regular hexagon

C
33cm
Regular octagon

4 What do 'penta', 'hexa' and 'octa' mean?

I These polygons have equal sides but they are not regular.

a Why not?   **b** Are they symmetrical?

c First estimate and then work out their perimeters in metres.

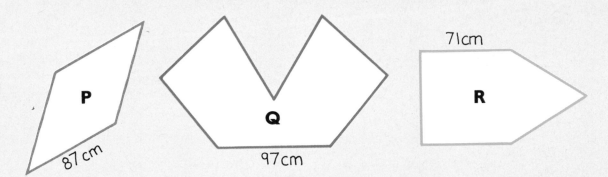

Sometimes measurements are given in metres and parts of a metre.
(Estimate 4+4+2+3 = 13m)

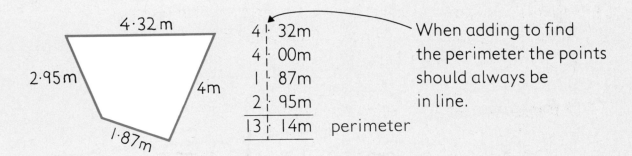

```
4 ¦ 32m
4 ¦ 00m
1 ¦ 87m
2 ¦ 95m
13 ¦ 14m   perimeter
```

When adding to find
the perimeter the points
should always be
in line.

2 Estimate and then find the perimeter of a pentagon whose sides are 3·25m, 4·03m, 2m, 3·87m and 2·60m.

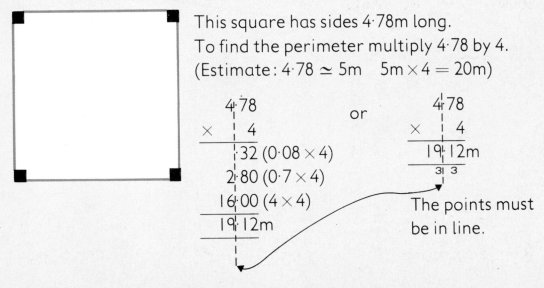

This square has sides 4·78m long.
To find the perimeter multiply 4·78 by 4.
(Estimate: 4·78 ≃ 5m   5m × 4 = 20m)

```
  4·78                       4·78
× ¦ 4          or          × ¦ 4
  ¦ 32 (0·08 × 4)           19¦ 12m
2¦ 80 (0·7 × 4)              3¦ 3
16¦ 00 (4 × 4)
19¦ 12m
```

The points must
be in line.

3 Estimate and then find the perimeter of a regular hexagon whose sides are 2·14 metres long.

Division of metres and centimetres

The perimeter of this square is 1·28m.
The sides are equal in length so to find
the length of one side, we divide the perimeter by 4.

1·28m ÷ 4 = 128cm ÷ 4

(Estimate: 'just over 120' ÷ 4
is 'just over 30',
so length of side ≃ 30cm.)

Length of side = 32cm or 0·32m.

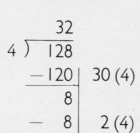

```
         32
  4 ) 128
    -120 |  30 (4)
       8
    -  8 |   2 (4)
   _____
        32
```

1 Find the lengths of sides of squares with these perimeters.
Give each answer first in cm then in m.

a 1·24m   **b** 2·88m   **c** 7·64m   **d** 4·04m   **e** 5·68m

2 For each of these regular polygons find the length of one side.
Give each answer first in cm then in m.

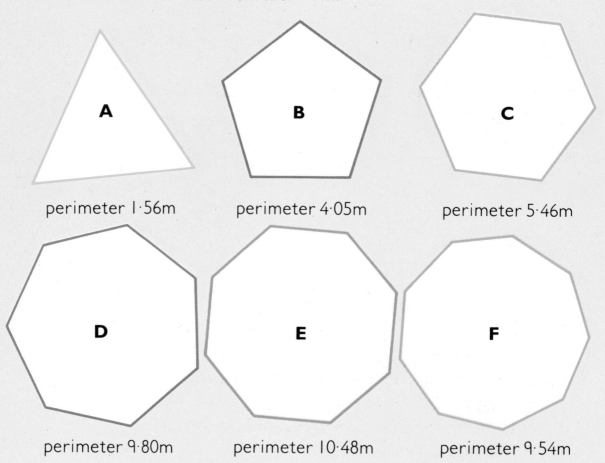

A perimeter 1·56m

B perimeter 4·05m

C perimeter 5·46m

D perimeter 9·80m

E perimeter 10·48m

F perimeter 9·54m

Jane cuts a rope, 13·80 metres long, into quarters to make four skipping ropes of equal length. How long is each skipping rope?

$\frac{1}{4}$ of 13·80 metres = 13·80 ÷ 4
(Estimate: 13·80m ≃ 14m; 14 ÷ 4 = $3\frac{1}{2}$.*)

First change 13·80m to cm then divide by 4.
Each skipping rope is 345cm or 3·45m long.

*(Was the estimate a good one?)

```
           345cm
   4 ) 1380cm
      −1200  300 (4)
        180
      − 160   40 (4)
         20
         20    5 (4)
             345 (4)
```

1 How long would each be if Jane wanted to make 5 equal skipping ropes from 13·80 metres?

2 How long is $\frac{1}{6}$ of 13·80 metres?

3 Give the answers to these in metres:

   a 10·43m ÷ 7   **c** 477cm ÷ 3   **e** 28·98m ÷ 9
   b 16·02m ÷ 6   **d** 11m ÷ 4   **f** 13dm ÷ 5

4 A loop of string is pegged out to make a regular hexagon with sides 1·25m long.

   a How long is the string?

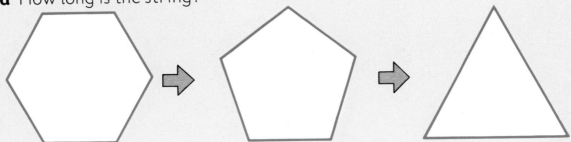

   b If the same loop is pegged out to make a regular pentagon, how long will one side be?
   c If an equilateral triangle is made from the same loop how long will its side be?
   d Compare the sides of the hexagon and the triangle. What do you notice?

Chapter 9: Money

1 Write the following amounts in pounds—the first is done for you.
  a 435p = £4·35   **c** 574p   **e** 891p   **g** 73p
  b 603p   **d** 306p   **f** 1024p   **h** 92p

2 Write the following amounts in pence:
  a £1·73   **c** £6·37   **e** £9·37   **g** £0·61
  b £3·49   **d** £8·94   **f** £10·61   **h** £0·17

3 Copy and add these amounts

	a £	**b** £	**c** £	**d** £
	4·73	3·61	1·94	3·42
	+2·69	+1·49	+6·87	+5·71
	1·58	7·82	7·82	3·94

The decimal points should always be beneath each other.

  e £3·72 + £1·96 + £5·83   **f** £4·91 + £1·37 + £6·73

4 Copy and subtract these amounts
  —the points should always be beneath each other:

a £	**b** £	**c** £	**d** £	**e** £	**f** £
6·73	3·96	4·23	3·91	6·23	8·02
−4·22	−1·43	−2·17	−1·88	−4·37	−4·80

Multiplication of £ by single digit

£3·62 × 7

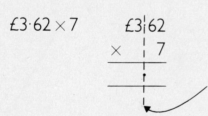

$$\begin{array}{r} £3·62 \\ \times\ \ \ \ 7 \\ \hline \end{array}$$

The points should always be beneath each other so first place the point in the answer line. Then multiply.

$$\begin{array}{r} £3·62 \\ \times\ \ \ \ 7 \\ \hline £25·34 \\ \hline {\scriptstyle 4\ 1} \end{array}$$

5 Multiply these in the same way
  a £1·32 × 3   **c** £3·51 × 5   **e** £4·78 × 8   **g** £2·19 × 8   **i** £5·87 × 9
  b £1·74 × 2   **d** £0·76 × 6   **f** £3·54 × 7   **h** £3·44 × 6   **j** £4·96 × 7
  k How much would you pay for five records if each one costs £3·59?
  l If you were given a £10 gift voucher to spend at a record shop, would
    you be able to buy four cassettes each costing £2·49?
  m What would it cost to rent a boat for seven days at £6·35 for a day?

Division by single digits

£8·96 ÷ 7

We write the amount without
its decimal point and divide
as we have done before:

```
        128
   7 ) 896
      -700 | 100 (7)
       196
      -140 | 20 (7)
        56
      - 56 | 8 (7)
            128 (7)
```

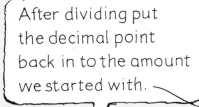

After dividing put
the decimal point
back in to the amount
we started with.

Following the rule
that decimal points
are in the same column
put a point in
the answer.
The answer is £1·28.

```
          1·28
   7 ) 8·96
      -700 | 100 (7)
       196
      -140 | 20 (7)
        56
      - 56 | 8 (7)
            128 (7)
```

l Divide these the same way:

a £5·25 ÷ 3	**d** £7·25 ÷ 3	**g** £9·14 ÷ 6	**j** £9·44 ÷ 8
b £2·78 ÷ 2	**e** £4·12 ÷ 3	**h** £6·36 ÷ 7	**k** £11·32 ÷ 10
c £6·36 ÷ 4	**f** £8·73 ÷ 5	**i** £10·12 ÷ 9	**l** £12·47 ÷ 8

m Three copies of a book cost £7·35. How much does each one cost?

n A boarding house charges £43·40 for a week's bed and breakfast.
What is the cost per day?

o How much does one shirt cost if I pay £20·85 for three?

p If I am paid £14·70 for 6 hours work, how much an hour is this?

1 Find the total cost of these using the prices
on the catalogue pages:

a Rubber torch   **b** Fork   **c** Shears
Sports bag   Spade   Watering can
Table tennis set _____   Rake _____   Hose _____

2 Which costs more and by how much?

a Vacuum flask or shears
b Table tennis set or sports bag
c Badminton racquet or wheelbarrow
d Lawn edger or rake

3 Find the cost of:

a 4 spades   **c** 6 hoses   **e** 8 vacuum flasks
b 3 sports bags   **d** 5 badminton racquets   **f** 7 shears

1 Copy and complete the following bills:

a 4 spades
   3 forks
   5 lawn edgers _____
   Total _____

b 5 table tennis sets
   7 badminton racquets
   4 sports bags _____
   Total _____

c 8 torches
   6 hoses
   5 watering cans _____
   Total _____

d 3 wheelbarrows
   6 shears
   5 rakes _____
   Total _____

2 If I buy 3 torches and a vacuum flask,
how much change should I get from a £10 note?

3 Here is a bill from last year.
What was the price last year for:

  a one torch.
  b one vacuum flask.
  c a sports bag.
  d one badminton racquet?

4 How much dearer is each item in
the bill this year?

5 Make out a similar bill using
this year's prices. How much
more is the total this year?

J. Bull & Co.

Hardware
~
Sports gear

8 High Street, Morpeth.

——— ◇ ———

5 torches	8·00
4 vacuum flasks	11·16
2 sports bags	9·98
3 badminton racquets	19·41
	£48·55

RECEIVED
WITH THANKS
14 May

J Bull

Chapter 10: Rounding off

Rulers, tape-measures, clock faces, protractors, measuring jars, dial scales etc. are all like a number line.
They have equally spaced marks to help us read off measurements.

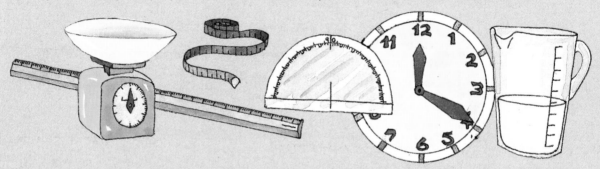

Sometimes a reading is between two marks.
To get an **approximate** answer we can **round up** or **round down** to the nearest mark.

> Approximate means 'close to' or 'nearly correct'.

Here is a part of a number line showing half-way marks between the whole numbers.

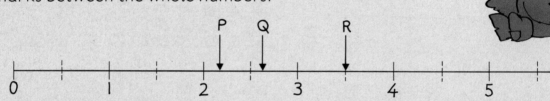

Because P is nearer to 2 than 3, it has an approximate reading of 2 to the nearest whole number (rounding down).

Q is nearer to 3 than 2; its approximate reading is 3 to the nearest whole number (rounding up).

R is on the half-way mark between 3 and 4. It is rounded up to the approximate reading of 4.

I Write the approximate reading, to the nearest whole number, for these letters:

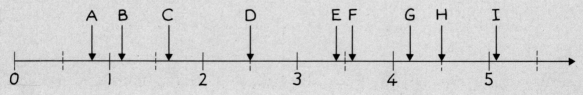

This diagram shows the rule for rounding up or rounding down.

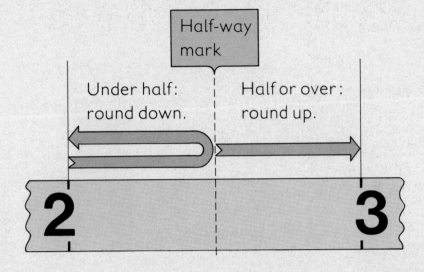

Half-way mark

Under half: round down.

Half or over: round up.

2 **3**

Some rulers are marked in half centimetres or in centimetres (cm) and millimetres (mm). 10mm = 1cm, so the half-way mark is 5mm along.

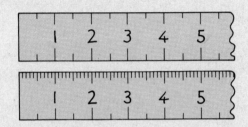

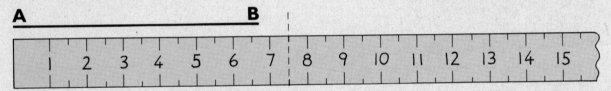

Line AB is 7cm *to the nearest centimetre.*
Line AB $\simeq$ 7cm. $\simeq$ means "is approximately equal to".

1 Measure these lines to the nearest cm. Use the $\simeq$ sign to record the lengths. The first one is done for you.

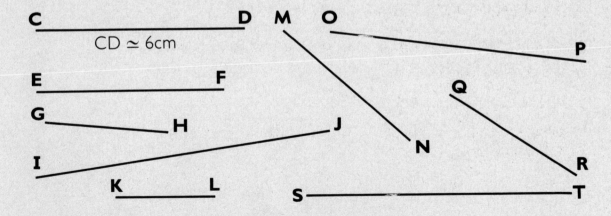

CD $\simeq$ 6cm

2 Measure the length and breadth of this book to the nearest centimetre.

These measuring jars are marked every 100 millilitres (ml).

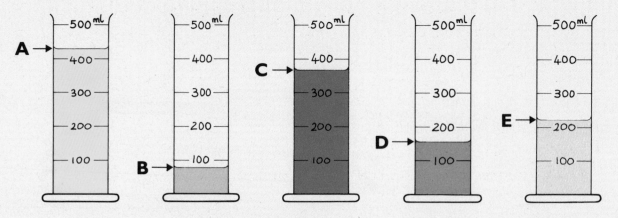

1 Write the amount in each jar to the nearest 100ml. Use the $\simeq$ sign.

Sometimes people give the approximate time shown on a clock. They often say, "It's just gone four o'clock" or "It's nearly ten past."

This clock shows:
six o'clock to the nearest hour.
 (nearer to six o'clock than 7);

half-past six to the nearest half-hour.
 (nearer to 6.30 than 6 o'clock);

quarter past six to the nearest quarter-hour.
 (nearer to $\frac{1}{4}$ past than $\frac{1}{2}$ past);

6.20 to the nearest 5 minutes.
 (nearer to 6.20 than 6.25).

2 Write the approximate time shown on clock, P

   a to the nearest hour.   **c** to the nearest $\frac{1}{4}$ hour.
   b to the nearest $\frac{1}{2}$ hour.   **d** to the nearest 5 minutes.

Do the same for clocks Q, R, S.

Rounding off decimal numbers

When rounding off decimal numbers to the nearest whole number,
0·5 is the half-way mark.

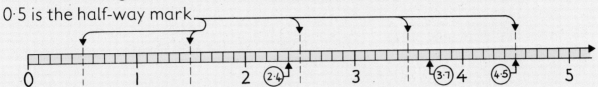

2·4 to the nearest whole number is 2·0 (rounding down).
3·7 to the nearest whole number is 4·0 (rounding up).
4·5 to the nearest whole number is 5·0 (rounding up).

1 Write these to the nearest whole number:

   a 2·7   **c** 26·9   **e** 7·5   **g** 9·6   **i** 7·06
   b 4·1   **d** 0·8   **f** 3·25   **h** 99·9   **j** 4·005

2 If lengths in m and cm are rounded off to the nearest metre,
   what is the half-way mark?

3 Write these lengths to the nearest metre:

   a 3m 15cm   **c** six and a half metres   **e** 375cm   **g** 13·26m
   b 7m 82cm   **d** 6·05 metres   **f** 68cm   **h** 29·85m

4 **a** Find the perimeter of this isosceles triangle.
   b Round off the perimeter to the nearest metre.
   c This time round off the length of each side
       to the nearest metre. Then add these rounded
       off lengths to find the perimeter in metres.
   d Compare your answers to **b** and **c**.
   Write a sentence about your results.

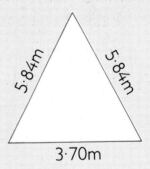

5 Make some measurements in your classroom and record them
   in a table like this:

distance	m	cm	approx. length to nearest metre
length of classroom breadth height of door			

Approximate area

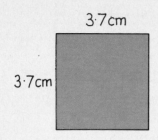

3·7cm

3·7cm

This square has sides 3·7cm long.
3·7cm ≃ 4cm to the nearest cm.
This square has an approximate area
of 4cm × 4cm, that is 16cm².

1 Calculate the approximate area of
these figures (not drawn to scale).
You must first round up or
round down as necessary.
Remember:
for less than ·5, round **down**
for ·5 or more, round **up**.

Muliply

2·3 cm

2·3 cm   **A**   1·6 cm

4·4cm

B

1·7cm

2·5 cm

2·5cm   **D**   3·6 cm

0·9 cm   **C**

7·2 cm

2 A piece of ribbon 2cm wide has an approximate area of 16cm² to
the nearest cm².
What is the shortest length it can have?

3 A small bedroom measures 3·8m wide and 5·2m long.
   a Would 15m² of carpet be sufficient to cover the floor?
   b What would be the least area of carpet, to the nearest m²,
   that you would need to buy?
   c Calculate the cost of the carpet at £9·50 per m².

4 Find the approximate areas (to the nearest square metre) of the floors
of rectangular rooms, corridors, etc. Record in a table like this:

	length m | cm	length to nearest m	breadth m | cm	breadth to nearest m	approx. area in m²
my bedroom	4 | 80	5 m	3 | 25	3 m	15 m²
classroom					

Approximate volume

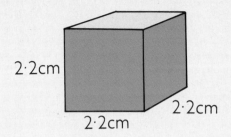

2·2cm
2·2cm
2·2cm

This cube has edges of 2·2cm.
2·2 ≃ 2cm (to the nearest cm).
The cube has an approximate volume
of 2cm × 2cm × 2cm, that is 8cm³.

1 Find the approximate volume of cubes with edges of:

a 1·9cm **b** 3·3cm **c** 9·6cm **d** 5·9cm **e** 4·5cm

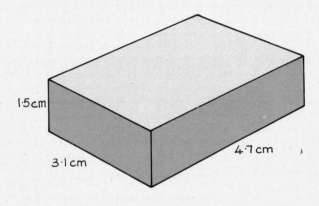

1·5cm
3·1cm
4·7cm

To find the approximate volume of
this cuboid, first round off
each measurement to nearest cm:

5cm × 3cm × 2cm

The approximate volume is 30cm³.

2 Find the approximate volume of each cuboid:

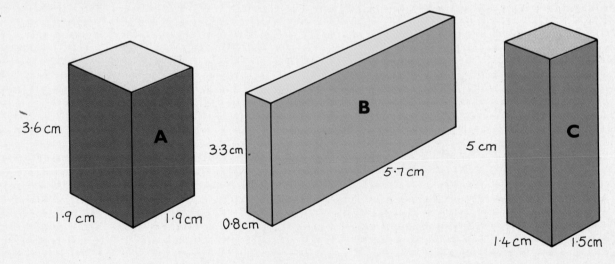

A
3·6 cm
1·9 cm 1·9 cm

B
3·3cm
5·7cm
0·8cm

C
5 cm
1·4 cm 1·5cm

3 Measure the length, breadth and height of your classroom to
the nearest metre. Find the approximate volume in m³.

Chapter 11: Area 2

Area of a triangle

1 On card carefully draw a rectangle
   6cm long and 3cm wide.

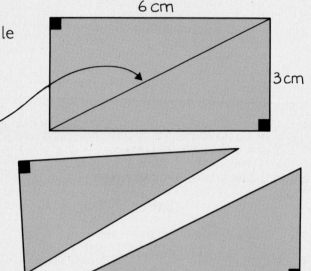

   a Write down the area
   of the rectangle.
   Draw a diagonal like this:
   Carefully cut out the rectangle.
   Now cut along the diagonal to
   make two right-angled triangles.
   A right-angle is marked
   like this:

   Check, without measuring, that the two triangles are the same size.

   b Write down the area of each triangle.

   c Copy and complete: The area of each triangle is [   ]
   the area of the rectangle.

2 Find the area of each of these triangles:

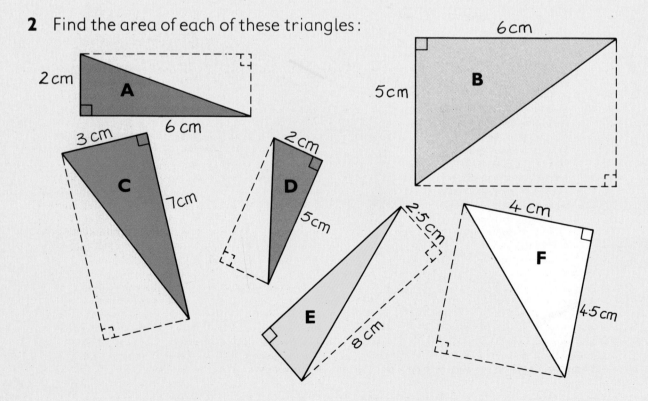

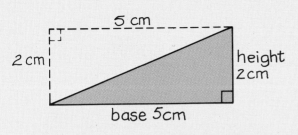

One side of this triangle, the **base**, is 5cm long.

The **height** of the triangle is always measured at right-angles to the **base**. It is the **perpendicular height**.

Area of **rectangle** is base × height
5cm × 2cm = 10cm²
Area of **triangle** is half the area of the rectangle
that is (base × height) ÷ 2
So the area of the **triangle** is 10cm² ÷ 2 = 5cm²

The area of a triangle is (base × height) ÷ 2

1 Find the areas of these right-angled triangles.
Set them out like the example: Area of triangle A = (b × h) ÷ 2
= (4 × 3) ÷ 2
= 12 ÷ 2
= 6cm²

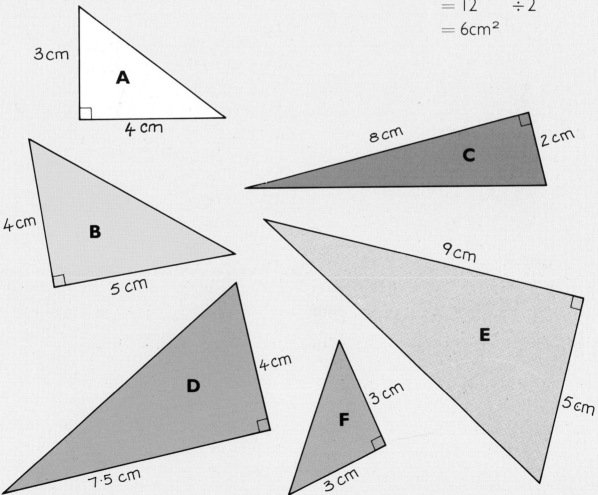

If a triangle is **not** right-angled, the height is still measured at **right-angles** to the base.

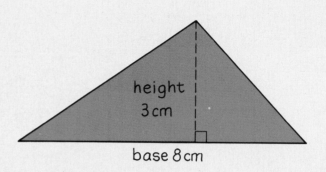

In this triangle:
    the base is 8cm and
    the perpendicular height is 3cm.

On cm-squared paper draw the triangle inside a rectangle like this:

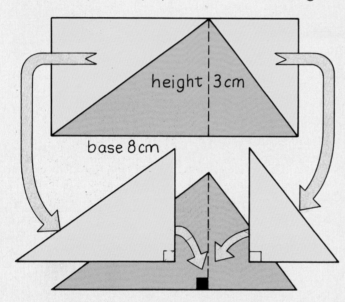

Cut out the rectangle. Then carefully cut off the two shaded triangles and turn them so that they fit together to cover the whole triangle.

The area of the brown triangle is **half** the area of the rectangle.
That is $(b \times h) \div 2$
$(8 \times 3) \div 2 = 24 \div 2 = 12$
Area of triangle is 12cm²

1 On squared paper draw these rectangles and triangles.
   Work out the area of each triangle.

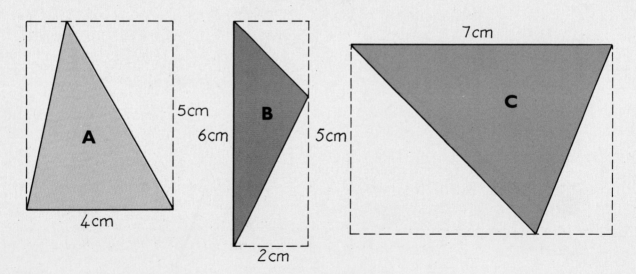

Chapter 9: Money

1 Write the following amounts in pounds—the first is done for you.

   a 435p = £4·35   **c** 574p   **e** 891p   **g** 73p

   b 603p   **d** 306p   **f** 1024p   **h** 92p

2 Write the following amounts in pence:

   a £1·73   **c** £6·37   **e** £9·37   **g** £0·61

   b £3·49   **d** £8·94   **f** £10·61   **h** £0·17

3 Copy and add these amounts

a £	**b** £	**c** £	**d** £
4·73	3·61	1·94	3·42
+2·69	+1·49	+6·87	+5·71
1·58	7·82	7·82	3·94

> The decimal points should always be beneath each other.

   e £3·72 + £1·96 + £5·83   **f** £4·91 + £1·37 + £6·73

4 Copy and subtract these amounts
—the points should always be beneath each other:

a £	**b** £	**c** £	**d** £	**e** £	**f** £
6·73	3·96	4·23	3·91	6·23	8·02
−4·22	−1·43	−2·17	−1·88	−4·37	−4·80

Multiplication of £ by single digit

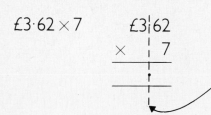

£3·62 × 7

$$\begin{array}{r} £3\!\cdot\!62 \\ \times \quad 7 \\ \hline \end{array}$$

> The points should always be beneath each other so first place the point in the answer line. Then multiply.

$$\begin{array}{r} £3\cdot62 \\ \times \qquad 7 \\ \hline £25\cdot34 \\ \hline \scriptstyle 4\ 1 \end{array}$$

5 Multiply these in the same way

   a £1·32 × 3   **c** £3·51 × 5   **e** £4·78 × 8   **g** £2·19 × 8   **i** £5·87 × 9

   b £1·74 × 2   **d** £0·76 × 6   **f** £3·54 × 7   **h** £3·44 × 6   **j** £4·96 × 7

   k How much would you pay for five records if each one costs £3·59?

   l If you were given a £10 gift voucher to spend at a record shop, would you be able to buy four cassettes each costing £2·49?

   m What would it cost to rent a boat for seven days at £6·35 for a day?

Jane cuts a rope, 13·80 metres long, into quarters
to make four skipping ropes of equal length.
How long is each skipping rope?

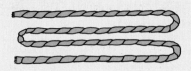

$\frac{1}{4}$ of 13·80 metres = 13·80 ÷ 4

(Estimate: 13·80m ≃ 14m; 14 ÷ 4 = $3\frac{1}{2}$.*)

First change 13·80m to cm then divide by 4.
Each skipping rope is 345cm or 3·45m long.

* (Was the estimate a good one?)

```
            345cm
    4 ) 1380cm
      −1200  300 (4)
         180
      − 160   40 (4)
          20
          20    5 (4)
              345 (4)
```

1 How long would each be if Jane wanted to make 5 equal skipping ropes
from 13·80 metres?

2 How long is $\frac{1}{6}$ of 13·80 metres?

3 Give the answers to these in metres:

    a 10·43m ÷ 7   **c** 477cm ÷ 3   **e** 28·98m ÷ 9

    b 16·02m ÷ 6   **d** 11m ÷ 4   **f** 13dm ÷ 5

4 A loop of string is pegged out to make a regular hexagon
with sides 1·25m long.

    a How long is the string?

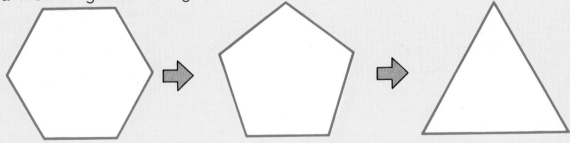

    b If the same loop is pegged out to make a regular pentagon,
how long will one side be?

    c If an equilateral triangle is made from the same loop
how long will its side be?

    d Compare the sides of the hexagon and the triangle.
What do you notice?

I Find the areas of these triangles. When the base or perpendicular height is not marked, measure it.

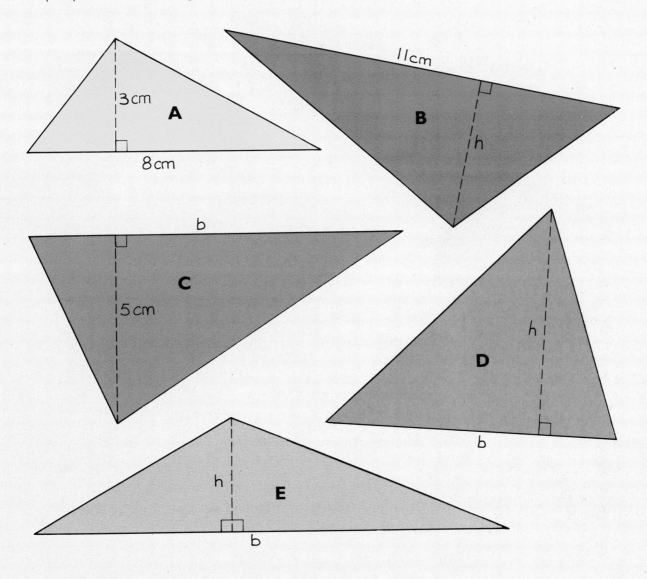

2 What is the area, in square metres, of the end wall of this house?

3 Find the area of this flower bed in m².

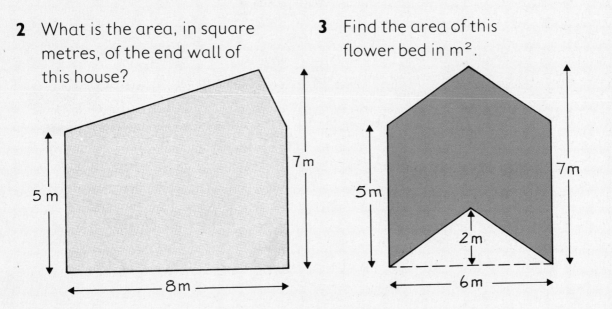

Chapter 12: Co-ordinates .

Plotting points

I   Copy this lattice on to centimetre squared paper using one square on
your paper for one square in the diagram.

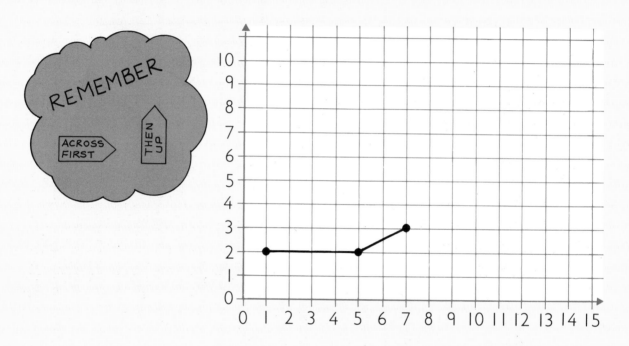

Mark and plot these points, joining them together as you plot them
(the first three are drawn for you):

(1,2); (5,2); (7,3); (9,3); (10,4); (12,4); (14,5); (12,6); (10,6); (9,7); (7,7);
(5,8); (1,8); (4,7); (4,3); (1,2).

2   Make another lattice on squared paper like the last one.
Mark and plot these points joining them together as you plot them.

(2,1); (2,6); (4,8); (6,8); (8,7); (10,8); (11,7); (12,4); (11,2); (10,2); (11,4);
(10,5); (9,4); (9,1); (8,1); (8,4); (6,3); (3,4); (3,1); (2,1).

Then join (2,6) to (1,5),
and join (9,5) to (7,5) to (9,7).
Put an eye at (10,6).

3   Make up a picture of your own. List the points in order and give it to
your friend for him to draw.

A straight line graph

$3 + 7 = 10$
$8 + 2 = 10$

These are two pairs of whole
numbers which add up to 10.
They can be written as:

(3,7); (8,2)

1 a Make a list of all the pairs
of numbers which add up to 10
—don't forget (0,10).

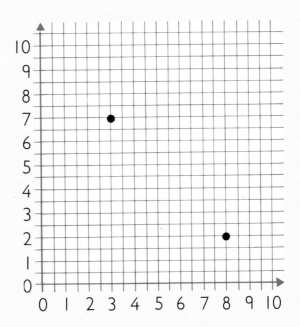

b Copy this lattice onto
centimetre squared paper
using a square centimetre
for each square in the diagram.
Notice that each number takes
two squares

c Plot the pairs of numbers you listed.
Two are done for you.

d The points you have marked should all lie on a straight line.
Draw the line.
The line is the graph of pairs of numbers which add up to ten.

e As two squares were used for one whole
number when we marked our lattice,
the squares between are used
for halves. Write them on your lattice
as in this diagram.

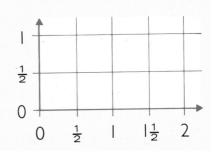

f Use the graph to complete these pairs of numbers which add up to 10:

$(7\frac{1}{2}, \square)$; $(\square, 3\frac{1}{2})$; $(1\frac{1}{2}, \square)$; $(5\frac{1}{2}, \square)$; $(\square, 9\frac{1}{2})$;

$(8\frac{1}{2}, \square)$; $(\square, 4\frac{1}{2})$.

Plotting shapes

1 a Copy the lattice in the diagram on to centimetre squared paper.

b Mark and join together, in order, the points:
(1,1); (5,1); (3,7); (1,1)

The shape drawn should be the isosceles triangle marked **a** on the diagram.

This shape has one axis of symmetry and it has been drawn on the figure with a dashed line.

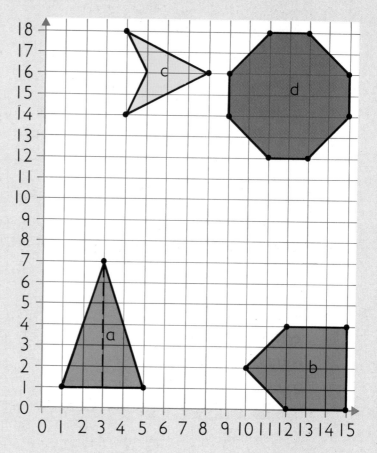

2 Copy the other three shapes onto the lattice making a list of the points plotted for each figure.
With a dashed line, mark in any axes of symmetry.

3 Plot these points joining them together in order.
Name the shape drawn and mark in any axes of symmetry.

a (1,13); (4,13); (4,10); (1,10); (1,13).

b (6,0); (9,0); (9,4); (6,4); (6,0).

c (12,7); (12,11); (15,10); (15,6); (12,7).

d (5,12); (6,14); (8,14); (9,12); (8,10); (6,10); (5,12).

e (5,6); (11,6); (9,9); (5,9); (5,6).

Translations

1 a Draw a lattice on centimetre
      squared paper. Number
      the horizontal —→ axis from
      0 to 10 and the vertical ↑ axis
      from 0–10.

   b Plot and join the points
      in order:
      A (1,1); B (1,4); C (4,4);
      D (4,1); A (1,1).

   c What shape have you drawn?

   d What is the area of the shape?

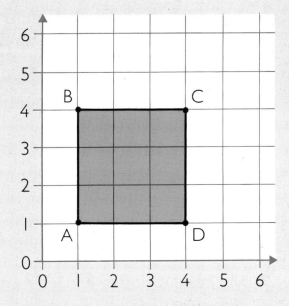

2 Adding 4 to the first number in each pair gives us a new set of points:

   Original set: A (1,1); B (1,4); C (4,4); D (4,1); A (1,1).

   New set: A (5,1); B (5,4); C (8,4); D (8,1); A (5,1).

   a Mark and join up the new set of points in a different colour.
   b What shape have you drawn?
   c What is its area?
   d What has happened to the original shape?

3 a Make a new set of points by adding 5 to the second number in each
      pair of the **original** set.
   b Mark and join up the new set of points in a different colour.
   c What shape have you drawn?
   d What is its area?
   e What has happened to it?

4 a Make a new set of points by adding 4 to the first number and by adding
      5 to the second number in each pair of the **original** set.
   b Mark and join up the new set of points in a different colour.
   c What shape have you drawn?
   d What is its area?
   e What has happened to it?

Enlargements

1 **a** Draw a lattice on centimetre-squared paper. Number the horizontal and vertical axes from 0 to 16.

   b Plot and join the points:
   A (1,1); B (1,4); C (2,4);
   D (4,2); E (4,1); A (1,1).

   c What is the area of the shape?

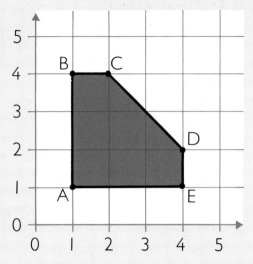

2 Multiplying both numbers in each pair by 3 gives a new set of points:

   Original set: A (1,1); B (1,4); C (2,4); D (4,2); E (4,1); A (1,1).

   New set: A (3,3); B (3,12); C (6, 12); D (12, 6); E (12, 3); A (3,3).

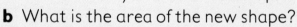

   a Mark, letter and join up with a different coloured crayon the new set of points.
   b What is the area of the new shape?
   c Multiplying the numbers by 3, multiplies the area by
   d Use a dashed line to join the two A's.
   e Do the same for each of the other letters.
   f Continue the dashed lines to the left. What happens?

3 **a** Multiply the original pairs by 2.
   b Mark, letter and join up with another coloured crayon the new set of points.
   c What do you notice about the new points?
   d What is the area of the new shape?
   e Multiplying the numbers by 2, multiplies the area by

4 **a** Multiply the original set by 4, plot and join up the points.
   b Multiplying the numbers by 4, multiplies the area by
   c Continue the dashed lines to the right. What happens?

Reflections

1 **a** Copy this lattice on to centimetre
      squared paper.
   b Plot these points:
      (4,4); (9,9); (1,1).
   c These points are on a straight
      line.
      Draw as much of the line
      as you can.
   d Using whole numbers only make
      a list of other points which are
      on the line.

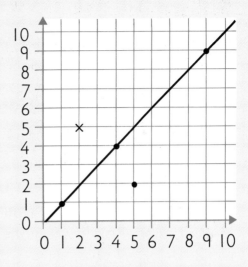

The point (5,2) has been marked on the lattice. If the line drawn
is a mirror line or an axis of symmetry, there will be a reflection
or matching point on the other side of the line. It is marked with
a cross at (2,5).

2 Plot these points with dots and mark their reflections
   with crosses:

   a (8,4)   **d** (9,2)   **g** (7,8)
   b (3,7)   **e** (1,6)   **h** (9,5)
   c (5,3)   **f** (0,4)   **i** (2,7)

3 **a** Copy the lattice above on to centimetre squared paper.
   b Draw in the reflection line.
   c Plot and join in order these points:
      A (3,1); B (7,2); C (5,2); D (6,4); A (3,1)
   d Draw the reflection of this shape.
   e Copy and complete:

      Original points: A (3,1); B (7,2); C (5,2); D (6,4); A (3,1).

      New points: A (,); B (,); C (,); D (,); A (,).

4 What do you notice about these reflections?

Chapter 13: Weight

Nett weight and gross weight

This tin of peas weighs 520g but the label says 425g.
This means that the peas inside the tin
weigh 425g—this is the nett weight.
The peas and the tin together weigh 520g—
this is called the gross weight.

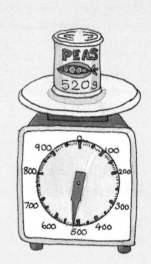

1 How much will the empty tin weigh?

2 a Copy and complete this table
for other tins of food.

b What is the total gross weight
of all five full tins?
(Answer first in g then in kg.)

c What is the weight of
the heaviest empty tin?

	Gross weight	Nett weight	Weight of tin
peaches	1025g	822g	
carrots	520g	425g	
soup	490g		55g
beans		576g	158g
salmon	260g		47g

3 a How many grams does each small marking on the dial stand for?

b The pointers show the gross weight
of some more goods.

Make another table like
the one in question 2.

Nett weights are shown
in brackets.

A Chocolates (120g).
B Jelly (180g).
C Crunchies (375g).
D Cornflakes (500g).
E Jam (454g).
F Pears (792g).

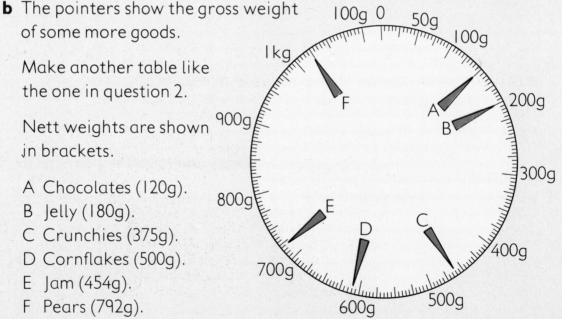

c What is the weight of the lightest container?

1000g = 1 kilogram.

'kilo' comes from a Greek word meaning 'a thousand'.

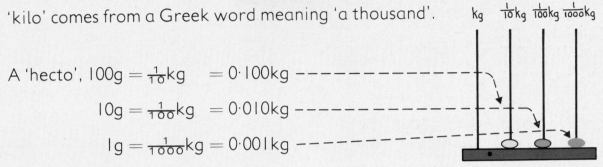

A 'hecto', $100g = \frac{1}{10}kg = 0.100kg$ - - - - - - - - - - - -

$10g = \frac{1}{100}kg = 0.010kg$ - - - - - - - - - - - -

$1g = \frac{1}{1000}kg = 0.001kg$ - - - - - - - - - - - -

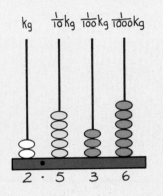

$2536g = 2000g + 500g + 30g + 6g$

$= 2kg + 0.500kg + 0.030kg + 0.006kg$

$= 2.536kg$

1 Draw abacus pictures of these weights and record them in kilograms:

   a 1234g   **c** 606g   **e** 4 hectos   **g** 15g

   b 325g   **d** 3030g   **f** half a kg   **h** 8g

2 Rewrite each of these lists so that the weights are in order with the heaviest at the top and the lightest at the bottom.
(Use the information at the top of this page to help you.)

a 30g	**b** 0·200kg	**c** 27g	**d** half a kg
$\frac{9}{10}kg$	$\frac{7}{100}kg$	$\frac{4}{100}kg$	$\frac{75}{100}kg$
0·060kg	19g	0·300kg	720g
50g	0·090kg	$\frac{2}{1000}kg$	7 'hectos'
4 'hectos'	60g	80g	0·725kg

3 Find the total of the weights in each list.

1

This cake weighs 2·270kg.

In an 'estimate the weight of the cake' competition, these weights were recorded:

A 2kg   E 2·500kg
B 1½kg   F 1700g
C 227g   G 22·700kg
D 1kg 900g   H 2kg 27g

a Which estimate is the 'winner'?
b Which is the second nearest?
c Write the estimates in order starting with the heaviest.
d How much heavier is the largest estimate than the smallest?

When rounding off weights to the nearest kilogram:

for 0·500kg and over, round **up**.
for less than 0·500kg, round **down**.

For example: 2·360kg ≃ 2kg; 3·635 ≃ 4kg

2 Write these weights to the nearest kg:

a 2·426kg   b 1·830kg   c 4·050kg   d 0·680kg   e 1245g

3 Rounding off to the nearest kilogram helps to work out the approximate total weight of several parcels.

a Add the rounded off weights of these five parcels to find the **approximate** total weight.

b Find the **actual** total weight.

c What is the difference between the two totals?

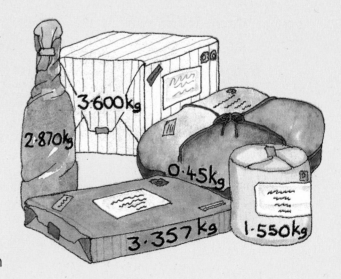

Multiplication of kg and g

The gross weight of
a tin of plums is 1·135kg.
To find the total weight
of 5 tins, multiply
1·135kg by 5.
(Estimate: 1·135kg × 5
≃ 5·500kg)

$$
\begin{array}{rl}
1\!\cdot\!135\text{kg} & \\
\times \quad 5 & \\
\hline
\cdot025 & (\cdot005 \times 5) \\
\cdot150 & (\cdot030 \times 5) \\
\cdot500 & (\cdot100 \times 5) \\
5\cdot000 & (1\cdot000 \times 5) \\
\hline
5\cdot675\text{kg} &
\end{array}
$$

or

$$
\begin{array}{r}
1\!\cdot\!135\text{kg} \\
\times \quad 5 \\
\hline
5\cdot675\text{kg} \\
\scriptstyle 1\;2
\end{array}
$$

The decimal
points
must be in line.

1 The nett weight of the plums in each tin is 937 grams.
   What is the total nett weight of the plums from 5 tins?

2 Find the difference between the total gross weight and the total nett
   weight of 7 tins of pears if 1 tin has a gross weight of 1·025 and a nett
   weight of 792g. (Estimate first.)

Division of kg and g

If 4 bottles of lemonade weigh 2·328kg what does 1 bottle weigh?
(Estimate: 2·400 ÷ 4 = 0·600, so 2·328kg ÷ 4 is just under 0·600)

Working in kilograms:

$$
\begin{array}{rl}
0\cdot582\text{kg} & \\
4\,\overline{)\ 2\cdot328\text{kg}} & \\
-2\cdot000 & \big|\ 0\cdot500 \times 4 \\
\hline
0\cdot328 & \\
-0\cdot320 & \big|\ 0\cdot080 \times 4 \\
\hline
0\cdot008 & \\
-0\cdot008 & \big|\ 0\cdot002 \times 4 \\
\hline
& \big|\ 0\cdot582\text{kg}
\end{array}
$$

or

Working in grams:

$$
\begin{array}{rl}
582\text{g} = 0\cdot582\text{kg} & \\
4\,\overline{)\ 2328\text{g}} & \\
-2000 & \big|\ 500 \times 4 \\
\hline
328 & \\
-\ 320 & \big|\ 80 \times 4 \\
\hline
8 & \\
-\ \ 8 & \big|\ 2 \times 4 \\
\hline
582\text{g} &
\end{array}
$$

3 Find the weight of 1 packet of soap-powder if the total weight of 6
   packets is 13·860kg.

4 5 tins of tomatoes weigh 3·695kg and 7 tins of beans weigh 5·075kg.
   Which is heavier, a tin of tomatoes or a tin of beans, and by how much?

Chapter 14: Fractions 1

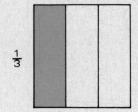 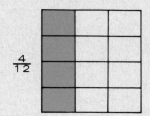 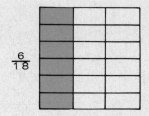

These diagrams show $\frac{1}{3}$, $\frac{4}{12}$ and $\frac{6}{18}$.
They are all members of the same family—the family of $\frac{1}{3}$.

1 a Draw diagrams to show $\frac{2}{6}$, $\frac{3}{9}$, $\frac{5}{15}$.
  b Do these three fractions belong to the family of $\frac{1}{3}$?

2 Copy and complete:
  a $7 \times 1 = \square$ **c** $1010 \times 1 = \square$ **e** $\frac{1}{5} \times 1 = \square$
  b $10 \times 1 = \square$ **d** $\frac{1}{2} \times 1 = \square$ **f** $\frac{1}{10} \times 1 = \square$

Multiplying a number by one leaves its value unchanged.

3 a $7 \div 1 = \square$ **c** $1010 \div 1 = \square$ **e** $\frac{1}{5} \div 1 = \square$
  b $10 \div 1 = \square$ **d** $\frac{1}{2} \div 1 = \square$ **f** $\frac{1}{10} \div 1 = \square$

Dividing a number by one leaves its value unchanged.

'The family of one'

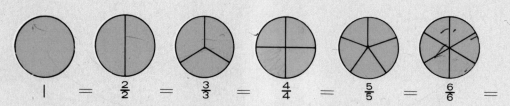

$1 \;=\; \frac{2}{2} \;=\; \frac{3}{3} \;=\; \frac{4}{4} \;=\; \frac{5}{5} \;=\; \frac{6}{6} \;=\;$

$\frac{1}{2} \times \left(\frac{3}{3}\right) = \frac{1 \times 3}{2 \times 3} = \frac{3}{6}$, so $\frac{1}{2} = \frac{3}{6}$

$\frac{1}{4} \times \left(\frac{5}{5}\right) = \frac{1 \times 5}{4 \times 5} = \frac{5}{20}$, so $\frac{1}{4} = \frac{5}{20}$

$\frac{20}{30} = \frac{2 \times 10}{3 \times 10} = \frac{2}{3} \times \left(\frac{10}{10}\right) = \frac{2}{3}$, so $\frac{20}{30} = \frac{2}{3}$

$\frac{18}{24} = \frac{3 \times 6}{4 \times 6} = \frac{3}{4} \times \left(\frac{6}{6}\right) = \frac{3}{4}$, so $\frac{18}{24} = \frac{3}{4}$

The value of a fraction is unchanged
if we multiply or divide
the numerator (number above the line)
and the denominator (number below
the line) by the same number.

Numerator $\longrightarrow$ $\dfrac{3}{4} = \dfrac{\square}{24}$

Denominator $\longrightarrow$

$\dfrac{3}{4} \overset{?}{\underset{\times 6}{=}} \dfrac{\square}{24}$

For these to be equal,
the numerator must be multiplied by 6
because the denominator has been multiplied by 6.

$\dfrac{3}{4} = \dfrac{3 \times 6}{4 \times 6} = \dfrac{\boxed{18}}{24}$

$\dfrac{15}{20} = \dfrac{3}{\square}$

$\dfrac{15}{20} \overset{\div 5}{\underset{?}{=}} \dfrac{3}{\square}$

The numerator has been divided by 5,
so the denominator must be divided by 5.

$\dfrac{15}{20} = \dfrac{(15 \div 5)}{(20 \div 5)} = \dfrac{3}{\boxed{4}}$

I Copy and complete:

a $\dfrac{3}{4} = \dfrac{\square}{8}$ f $\dfrac{70}{100} = \dfrac{\square}{10}$ k $\dfrac{2}{5} = \dfrac{\square}{35}$ p $\dfrac{32}{40} = \dfrac{4}{\square}$

b $\dfrac{8}{12} = \dfrac{2}{\square}$ g $\dfrac{3}{5} = \dfrac{9}{\square}$ l $\dfrac{12}{28} = \dfrac{\square}{7}$ q $\dfrac{5}{8} = \dfrac{30}{\square}$

c $\dfrac{4}{5} = \dfrac{16}{\square}$ h $\dfrac{12}{16} = \dfrac{3}{\square}$ m $\dfrac{1}{2} = \dfrac{\square}{32}$ r $\dfrac{35}{50} = \dfrac{\square}{10}$

d $\dfrac{21}{28} = \dfrac{\square}{4}$ i $\dfrac{3}{10} = \dfrac{9}{\square}$ n $\dfrac{36}{42} = \dfrac{6}{\square}$ s $\dfrac{7}{8} = \dfrac{\square}{56}$

e $\dfrac{2}{3} = \dfrac{18}{\square}$ j $\dfrac{22}{33} = \dfrac{2}{\square}$ o $\dfrac{5}{8} = \dfrac{\square}{24}$ t $\dfrac{27}{45} = \dfrac{\square}{5}$

I For each diagram write down the fraction shaded and the name of the family to which the fraction belongs:

Example: 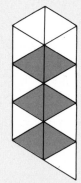 Fraction shaded $\frac{2}{6}$
Fraction family $\frac{1}{3}$

a

b

c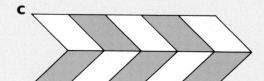

d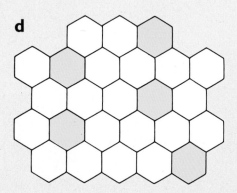

e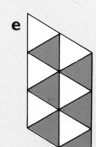

f

Addition

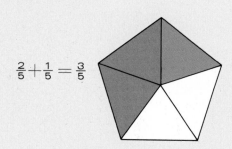

$\frac{2}{5} + \frac{1}{5} = \frac{3}{5}$

This is easy because we are thinking of 'fifths' and adding 'two fifths' to 'one fifth' to make 'three fifths'.

2 Copy and complete:

a $\frac{4}{7} + \frac{2}{7} = \square$

b $\frac{3}{8} + \frac{4}{8} = \square$

c $\frac{\square}{6} + \frac{5}{6} = 1$

d $\frac{2}{9} + \frac{4}{9} + \frac{1}{9} = \square$

e $\frac{2}{11} + \frac{\square}{11} = \frac{9}{11}$

f $\frac{4}{13} + \frac{1}{13} + \frac{\square}{13} = \frac{8}{13}$

Subtraction

This is also easy when we are comparing the same kind of things.

e.g. $\frac{4}{7} - \frac{1}{7} = \frac{3}{7}$ 　　　We compare 'one-seventh' with 'four-sevenths'— it is 'three-sevenths' less.

1 Copy and complete:

a $\frac{5}{8} - \frac{3}{8} = \square$ 　　　**d** $\frac{4}{7} - \frac{2}{7} = \square$ 　　　**g** $\frac{7}{9} - \frac{2}{9} = \square$

b $\frac{\square}{6} - \frac{1}{6} = \frac{4}{6}$ 　　　**e** $\frac{7}{11} - \frac{2}{11} - \frac{1}{11} = \square$ 　　　**h** $\frac{11}{12} - \frac{10}{12} = \square$

c $\frac{7}{12} - \frac{5}{12} = \frac{\square}{12}$ 　　　**f** $\frac{7}{10} - \frac{3}{10} = \frac{\square}{10}$ 　　　**i** $\square - \frac{2}{9} = \frac{4}{9}$

2 **a** $\frac{7}{9} - \frac{2}{9} + \frac{4}{9} = \frac{\square}{9} = \square$ 　　　**c** $\frac{5}{12} + \frac{6}{12} - \frac{8}{12} = \frac{\square}{12} = \frac{1}{\square}$

　　b $\frac{17}{20} - \frac{11}{20} = \frac{\square}{20} = \frac{3}{\square}$ 　　　**d** $\frac{5}{8} - \frac{1}{8} = \frac{\square}{8} = \frac{1}{\square}$

Different denominators

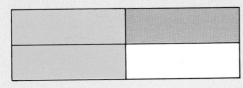

The diagram shows 　$\frac{1}{2} + \frac{1}{4} = \frac{3}{4}$

It is set down as: 　$\frac{1}{2} + \frac{1}{4} = \frac{2}{4} + \frac{1}{4}$

　　　　　　　　　　　$= \frac{3}{4}$

This diagram shows $\frac{4}{5} - \frac{3}{10}$

It is set down as: 　$\frac{4}{5} - \frac{3}{10} = \frac{8}{10} - \frac{3}{10}$

　　　　　　　　　　　$= \frac{5}{10}$

　　　　　　　　　　　$= \frac{1}{2}$

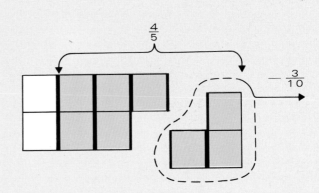

3 Do these in the same way:

a $\frac{1}{6} + \frac{5}{12}$ 　　**c** $\frac{2}{3} - \frac{1}{12}$ 　　**e** $\frac{7}{8} - \frac{11}{16}$ 　　**g** $\frac{9}{10} - \frac{2}{5}$ 　　**i** $\frac{2}{3} + \frac{1}{6}$

b $\frac{1}{2} + \frac{5}{16}$ 　　**d** $\frac{4}{5} - \frac{7}{10}$ 　　**f** $\frac{2}{3} + \frac{2}{15}$ 　　**h** $\frac{3}{8} + \frac{5}{16}$ 　　**j** $\frac{3}{4} - \frac{1}{16}$

$\frac{1}{2} + \frac{1}{3}$ is more difficult.

To find the common denominator we must look at the families of $\frac{1}{2}$ and $\frac{1}{3}$.

The family of $\frac{1}{2} = \left\{ \frac{1}{2}, \frac{2}{4}, \frac{3}{6}, \frac{4}{8}, \frac{5}{10}, \cdots \right\}$

The family of $\frac{1}{3} = \left\{ \frac{1}{3}, \frac{2}{6}, \frac{3}{9}, \frac{4}{12}, \frac{5}{15}, \cdots \right\}$

Looking along the lines we see that sixths are in both families.

$$\frac{1}{2} + \frac{1}{3} = \frac{3}{6} + \frac{2}{6}$$
$$= \frac{5}{6}$$

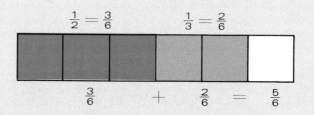

The family of $\frac{3}{5} = \left\{ \frac{3}{5}, \frac{6}{10}, \frac{9}{15}, \frac{12}{20}, \cdots \right\}$

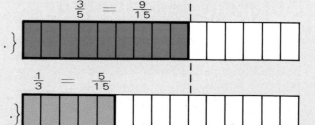

The family of $\frac{1}{3} = \left\{ \frac{1}{3}, \frac{2}{6}, \frac{3}{9}, \frac{4}{12}, \frac{5}{15}, \cdots \right\}$

$$\frac{3}{5} - \frac{1}{3}$$
$$= \frac{9}{15} - \frac{5}{15}$$
$$= \frac{4}{15}$$

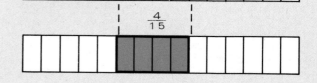

I Do these the same way.

a $\frac{1}{2} + \frac{1}{5}$ **d** $\frac{3}{4} - \frac{2}{3}$ **g** $\frac{3}{10} + \frac{2}{3}$ **j** $\frac{8}{9} - \frac{3}{4}$

b $\frac{1}{4} - \frac{1}{6}$ **e** $\frac{3}{8} + \frac{1}{3}$ **h** $\frac{7}{8} - \frac{2}{3}$ **k** $\frac{2}{5} + \frac{1}{4}$

c $\frac{2}{3} + \frac{1}{5}$ **f** $\frac{9}{10} - \frac{3}{4}$ **i** $\frac{2}{5} + \frac{1}{6}$ **l** $\frac{3}{4} - \frac{3}{5}$

Chapter 15: Graphs

1 This graph shows how many people attended the school play each night. The hall will hold 100 people. Tickets were 30p for adults and 20p for children.

  a How many more were at the play on Friday than on Tuesday?

  b Which was the most popular night?

  c Which was the least popular night?

  d What was the total attendance for the five nights?

  e What fraction of the hall was full on Tuesday night?

  f What fraction of the hall was empty on Monday night?

  g If 32 children were at the play on Friday what was the total amount of money taken on Friday?

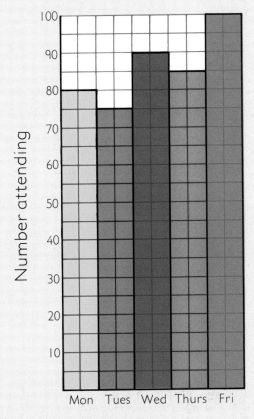

Graph showing attendance at school play.

2 a This table shows attendances each night. Copy and complete it.

Attendances	Monday	Tuesday	Wednesday	Thursday	Friday
Adults			59	58	
Children	30	28			32

  b What were the total receipts for the week?

3 Use these figures to draw a graph like the one above.

Attendances out of 32 for class 4	Monday		Tuesday		Wednesday		Thursday		Friday	
	a.m.	p.m.	a.m.	p.m.	a.m.	p.m.	a.m.	p.m.	a.m.	p.m.
	26	27	27	27	29	30	31	29	32	32

When you have drawn it make up some problems like those in question 1.

The table shows a tally of the number of pets owned by third year children.

Each mark represents 1 pet, ⊣⊦⊦ represents 5 pets.

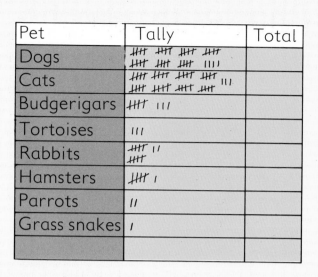

Pet	Tally	Total
Dogs	⊣⊦⊦ ⊣⊦⊦ ⊣⊦⊦ ⊣⊦⊦ ⊣⊦⊦ ⊣⊦⊦ ⊣⊦⊦ IIII	
Cats	⊣⊦⊦ ⊣⊦⊦ ⊣⊦⊦ ⊣⊦⊦ ⊣⊦⊦ ⊣⊦⊦ ⊣⊦⊦ ⊣⊦⊦ III	
Budgerigars	⊣⊦⊦ III	
Tortoises	III	
Rabbits	⊣⊦⊦ II ⊣⊦⊦	
Hamsters	⊣⊦⊦ I	
Parrots	II	
Grass snakes	I	

1 Copy the table and fill in the total numbers.

2 As there are eight different types of pet, draw the horizontal axis 16cm long so that each block will be 2cm wide.

There are more cats than any other pet so the tallest column will represent 43.

1cm represents 2 pets. Label both axes and give the graph a title.

3 Write three sentences about what the graph shows.

4 Make up three questions about the graph for your friends.

5 Choose other topics to investigate, collect the figures, make the tables and draw graphs of your results.

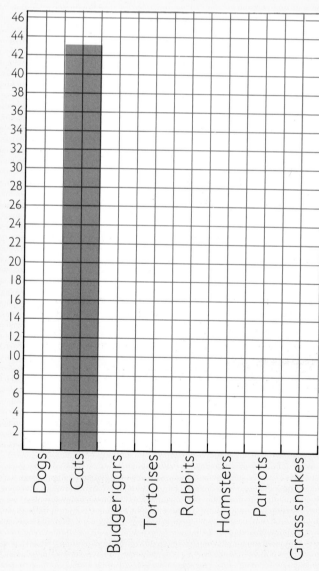

Pets owned by 3rd year pupils

Temperature graphs

The following table gives the average maximum temperatures in °C for London.

Jan	Feb	Mar	Apl	May	June	July	Aug	Sept	Oct	Nov	Dec
6	7	10	13	17	20	22	21	19	14	10	7

These can be shown on a graph.

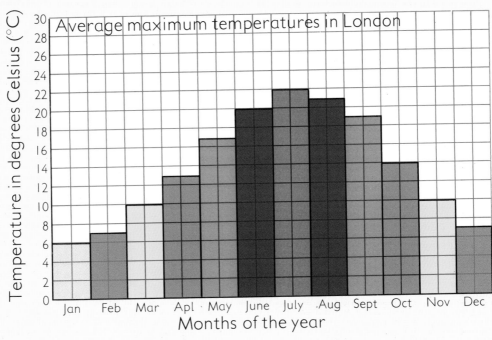

1 Which month had the highest temperature and which the lowest?
2 The difference between the highest and lowest temperatures is called the **range**. What is the range of temperatures in London?
3 Which months have the same temperatures?

A travel magazine gives the average maximum temperatures in °C for 3 Greek islands as :

	Jan	Feb	Mar	Apl	May	June	July	Aug	Sept	Oct	Nov	Dec
Limnos	11	12	13	18	23	27	30	30	26	22	16	13
Naxos	15	15	16	20	23	26	27	28	26	24	20	17
Zakynthos	14	14	16	20	25	29	32	32	29	25	20	16

4 Using a scale of 2cm for each month on the horizontal axis and 1cm for 2°C on the vertical axis, draw a separate graph for each island.

5 What is the range of temperatures for each island?

6 Which months in London are colder than the lowest month in Naxos?

7 How much warmer than London is Zakynthos in August?

Conversion graphs

In Britain the unit of currency is the pound (£). Other countries have different units of currency. In Upper Mathematica the unit of currency is the mult (mu). A visitor from Britain, last year, received 8mu for each £1.

The graph shows this conversion. The pounds have been marked on the horizontal axis and the mults on the vertical axis.

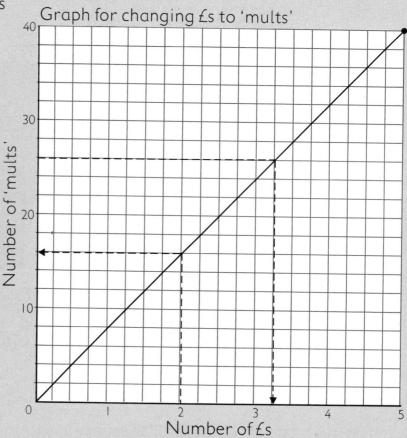

Graph for changing £s to 'mults'

1 How many squares are there for each £1?

2 How much is each square worth?

3 How many squares are there for ten mults?

4 How many mults is each square worth?

The broken line shows how to change £2 to mults. From £2 on the horizontal axis we go up to the conversion line and then read across to the mults column. £2 = 16mu.

To change 26mu to £ we follow the dotted line from 26mu across to the line and then down to the £ axis. 26mu = £3·25.

5 Convert these £ to mults:
   a £3   c £2·50   e £1·50   g £4·25
   b £5   d £3·50   f £3·75   h £2·75

6 Convert these mults to £:
   a 20mu   c 36mu   e 38mu   g 37mu
   b 30mu   d 42mu   f 46mu   h 25mu

Visitors to Upper Mathematica this year found that
they received 10 mults for £1.

1 Copy and complete:
   a £1 = 10mu   **c** £3 = ☐   **e** £5 = ☐
   b £2 = ☐   **d** £4 = ☐   **f** £0 = ☐

2 Draw axes as in the previous conversion graph but make the vertical
   axis taller, taking it to 50 mults.

3 Plot the points in question 1 and join them with a straight line.

4 Using your graph, copy and complete this table:

£	1		4		1·50		2·75		4·75	
mults	30		50		35		$32\frac{1}{2}$		$37\frac{1}{2}$

To exchange larger amounts than £5 we can either say:
   £11 = £5+£5+£1 = 50mu+50mu+10mu = 110mu
   or £18 = 6×£3   = 6×30mu   = 180mu

5 Using your graph copy, complete this table:

£	7	9	13	15	24	30
Mults						

6 Last year I bought a map in Upper Mathematica for 12mu.
   How many £ was that? (Use last year's graph!)

7 This year it is still 12mu. What would I have saved in £ if I had bought it
   this year?

8 A meal cost me 32mu last year. If the price is still the same this year
   what do I save in £ if I have a similar meal?

9 When I went to Upper Mathematica last year my holiday cost me 1 856
   mults. How many pounds was equal to that amount?
   If my holiday this year will cost the same number of mults how many
   pounds will it cost?
   What amount (in pounds) do I save this year?

A different sort of graph—a nomograph

This graph is designed to help us to add or subtract.

1 On centimetre squared paper draw three vertical lines each 20cm long and 3cm apart. Letter them **A**, **B** and **C**.

2 Number them as in the diagram with 2cm for each unit on the **A** and **C** columns and 1cm for each unit on the **B** column.

3 To add 5 and 4 place a ruler across the chart (see diagram) from 5 in column **A** to 4 in column **C**. The answer 9 is in the middle column.

4 Use the nomogram to complete:

a $1+2=$ f $4\frac{1}{2}+3\frac{1}{2}=$
b $3+5=$ g $7+2\frac{1}{2}=$
c $7+2=$ h $3\frac{1}{2}+5=$
d $3\frac{1}{2}+2\frac{1}{2}=$ i $6\frac{1}{2}+1=$
e $6\frac{1}{2}+\frac{1}{2}=$ j $5\frac{1}{2}+2\frac{1}{2}=$

5 Look at the broken line.
Can you see how we could read $9-5=4$?
Which column is the answer in?

6 Complete using the nomogram:

a $7-5=$ e $8\frac{1}{2}-3\frac{1}{2}=$
b $8-2=$ f $6\frac{1}{2}-5\frac{1}{2}=$
c $6-4=$ g $8-3\frac{1}{2}=$
d $7\frac{1}{2}-2\frac{1}{2}=$ h $6\frac{1}{2}-4=$

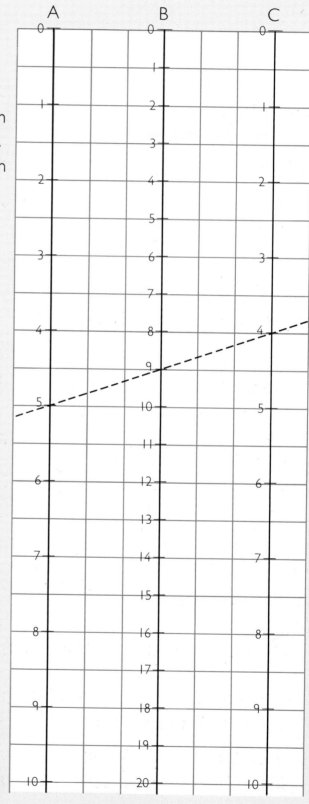

Chapter 16: Multiplication 2

Multiplication by 10 and 100

1 Copy and complete

a $4 \times 10 =$ **c** $8 \times 10 =$ **e** $6 \times 10 =$ **g** $7 \times 10 =$

b $3 \times 10 =$ **d** $5 \times 10 =$ **f** $9 \times 10 =$ **h** $10 \times 10 =$

 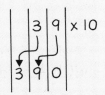

> To multiply a number by 10:
> move the digits **one** column to the left
> and put a zero in the empty units space.

2 **a** $12 \times 10 =$ **d** $19 \times 10 =$ **g** $60 \times 10 =$ **j** $100 \times 10 =$

b $15 \times 10 =$ **e** $26 \times 10 =$ **h** $91 \times 10 =$ **k** $130 \times 10 =$

c $21 \times 10 =$ **f** $40 \times 10 =$ **i** $203 \times 10 =$ **l** $700 \times 10 =$

To multiply by multiples of 10 (20, 30, 40, 50, . . . etc.)
first multiply the digits then use the rule to multiply by 10.

$$8 \times 40 = \quad 8 \times 4 \times 10 \qquad\qquad 63 \times 20 = \quad 63 \times 2 \times 10$$
$$= \quad 32 \times 10 \longleftarrow \text{1st step} \qquad = 126 \times 10 \longleftarrow \text{1st step}$$
$$= \quad 320 \quad \longleftarrow \text{2nd step} \qquad = 1260 \quad \longleftarrow \text{2nd step}$$

3 **a** 4×20 **d** 12×30 **g** 32×70 **j** 30×20

b 7×50 **e** 14×60 **h** 46×50 **k** 40×40

c 8×90 **f** 24×40 **i** 87×30 **l** 80×70

> To multiply a number by 100:
> move the digits **two** columns to the left and
> put zeros in the empty units and tens columns.

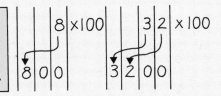

4 **a** 4×100 **c** 13×100 **e** 23×100 **g** 40×100

b 6×100 **d** 27×100 **f** 89×100 **h** 70×100

To multiply by multiples of 100 (200, 300, 400, . . . etc.)
first multiply the digits then use the rule to multiply by 100.

5 **a** 4×200 **c** 13×400 **e** 23×600 **g** 29×700

b 7×500 **d** 32×800 **f** 41×500 **h** 95×200

Here is a diagram which shows 16 × 14

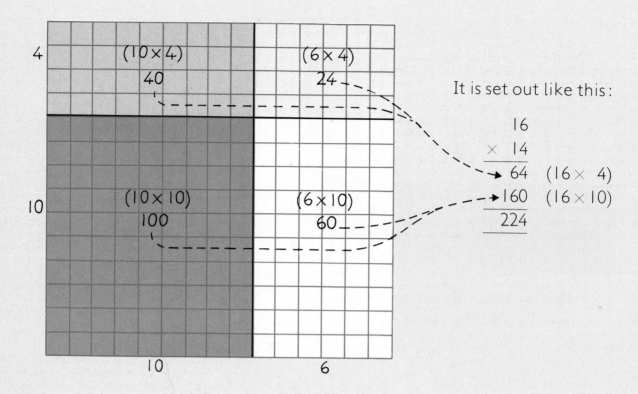

It is set out like this:

```
      16
    × 14
    ————
      64   (16 × 4)
     160   (16 × 10)
     ————
     224
```

Do these in the same way. Draw a diagram for each and set it out like the example.

1 **a** 13   **b** 14   **c** 15   **d** 16   **e** 19
        ×12   ×13   ×12   ×15   ×18

2 Try to do these without a diagram. The first is done for you.

a   14   **c**   15   **e**   18   **g**   16   **i**   18
        × 12   ×13   ×13   ×14   ×16
        ————
         28   (14 × 2)
        140   (14 × 10)
        ————
        168

b   15   **d**   14   **f**   16   **h**   17   **j**   19
        ×14   ×14   ×16   ×16   ×19

This diagram shows 38 × 27

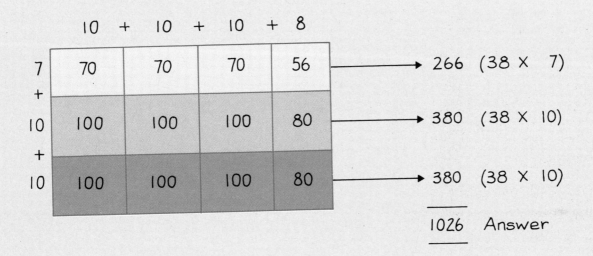

	10 +	10 +	10 +	8			
7 +	70	70	70	56	→	266	(38 × 7)
10 +	100	100	100	80	→	380	(38 × 10)
10	100	100	100	80	→	380	(38 × 10)
						1026	Answer

We do not need to draw these exactly —
a sketch will do.

34 × 22

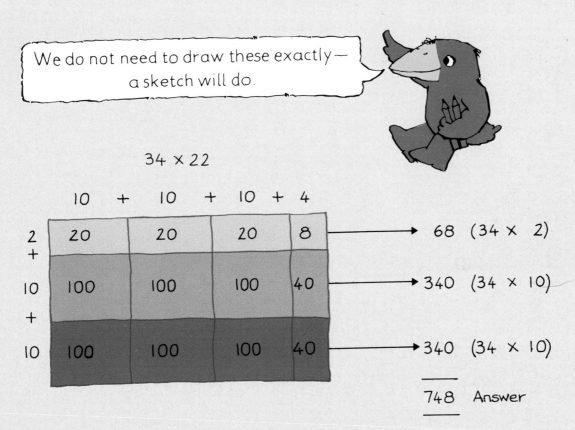

	10 +	10 +	10 +	4			
2 +	20	20	20	8	→	68	(34 × 2)
10 +	100	100	100	40	→	340	(34 × 10)
10	100	100	100	40	→	340	(34 × 10)
						748	Answer

1 Do these in the same way:

a 23 × 17 **d** 25 × 23 **g** 52 × 37 **j** 58 × 51

b 45 × 14 **e** 29 × 21 **h** 46 × 34 **k** 69 × 62

c 37 × 19 **f** 46 × 28 **i** 62 × 43 **l** 78 × 59

Here is a plan divided into fewer parts. It shows 37×26.

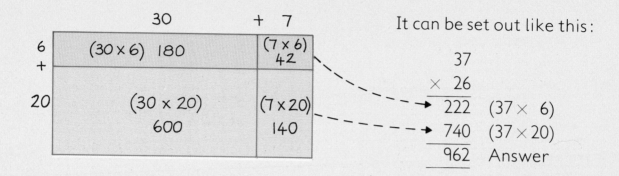

It can be set out like this:

```
        37
     ×  26
       222   (37 ×  6)
       740   (37 × 20)
       962   Answer
```

1 Do these in the same way:

  a 34×24 **b** 39×26 **c** 59×52 **d** 79×63

2 Try these without a diagram. The first is done for you.

  a
```
        43
     ×  37
       301   (43 ×  7)
      1290   (43 × 30)
      1591
```

  b 47×33 **g** 85×64
  c 67×56 **h** 65×39
  d 29×29 **i** 94×87
  e 53×34 **j** 75×42
  f 73×59 **k** 93×34

3 **a** If there are 28 children in each class, how many will there be in 16 classes?

  b The seats for a concert are set out in rows of 32. If there is room for 18 rows, how many tickets can be sold?

  c What is the product of 43 and 27?

  d John's friends promise to give him 35p for every length he completes in a sponsored swim. If he swims 22 lengths, how much money should he receive?

  e How many nails will be needed to make 24 geoboards if there are 36 nails in each?

  f Find the floor area in m² of a rectangular hall which is 29m long and 21m wide.

  g 1, 4, 9, 16, 25, 36, 49, 64, 81 and 100 are the first 10 square numbers. Work out the next 10 square numbers up to 400. Check your result by studying the pattern.

  h Start by working out 35×35, then 36×34, then 37×33, then 38×32, and so on. Look for the pattern made by the products.

Chapter 17: Shape 2

Quadrilaterals

A quadrilateral is a four-sided figure.

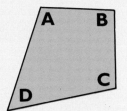

1   Draw any quadrilateral on a piece of paper and mark its angles **A**, **B**, **C**, **D** as in the diagram. Cut it out.

2   Tear off the four angles as shown.

3   Fit them together like this:

The four angles of a quadrilateral add up to 360°.

4   Calculate the size, in degrees, of the lettered angles in these quadrilaterals.

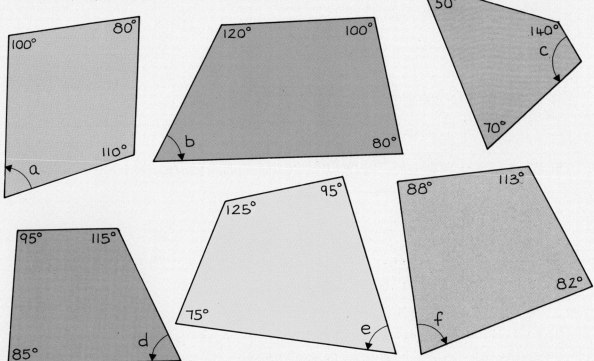

Some special quadrilaterals

Copy these quadrilaterals on to centimetre-squared paper.
Draw in the diagonals as in the diagram.
Cut out the shapes.

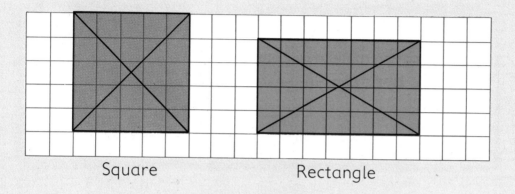

Square   Rectangle

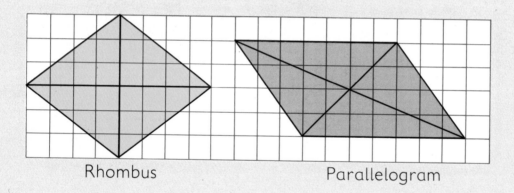

Rhombus   Parallelogram

I Copy and complete this table:

	Square	Rhombus	Rectangle	Parallel-ogram
Four sides of a quadrilateral equal?			No	
Four angles of a quadrilateral equal?	Yes			
Diagonals same length?		No		
Do diagonals cut each other in half?				
Do diagonals cross at right angles?				
Are diagonals axes of symmetry?				
Are the angles of the quadrilateral cut in half by the diagonals?	Yes			

1 Copy these shapes carefully on to squared paper.

Mark all right angles like this:

Mark angles which are equal in the same colour:

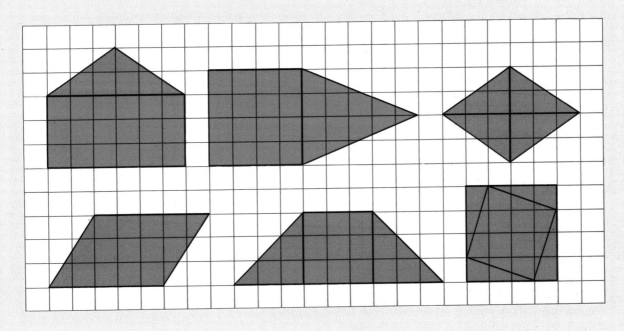

2 Find the size of each lettered angle in these diagrams:

Where lines are marked it means they are equal.

Remember: the 3 angles of a triangle together make 180°.

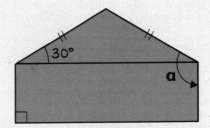

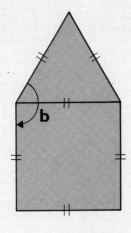

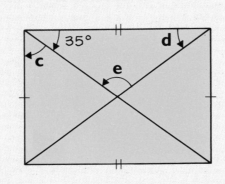

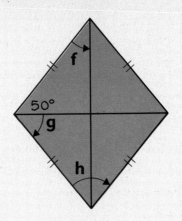

Tessellation

Some shapes fit together without gaps between them.
This is called tessellation. (The Latin word *tessella* means a tile.)
Look around for floors, walls or pathways that are covered
by tiles or slabs.

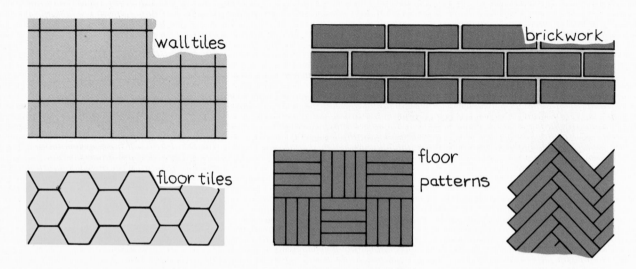

Cut out some 'tiles' from card or sticky paper, making sure the tiles in each
set are of the same shape and size.
You may have plastic shapes you can use.

Try sets of (**a**) equilateral, (**b**) right-angled, (**c**) scalene triangles
to see if they tessellate.

 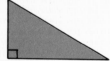 

Squares and rectangles tessellate.
Now try other quadrilaterals
to see if they tessellate.

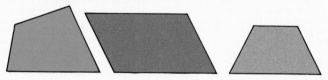

If 3 different colours are used,
the tessellation pattern of
a rhombus can be made to look
as though it is formed by cubes.
Try this for yourself.

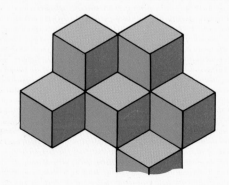

Chapter 18: Division 2

In Chapter 16 we learned how to multiply by ten and multiples of ten.

To multiply by 100 we move digits
2 columns to the left and fill
the tens and units spaces with zeros.

| | | 7 | × 100
|7|0|0|

| | | 3 | 4 | × 100
|3|4|0|0|

1 Copy and complete these:

a 4 × 100 =   **c** 12 × 100 =   **e** 39 × 100 =   **g** 73 × 100 =
b 9 × 100 =   **d** 27 × 100 =   **f** 48 × 100 =   **h** 86 × 100 =

Multiplication by multiples of 100 is carried out in two steps:
For example: 34 × 600

34 × 6 × 100
204 × 100
20400

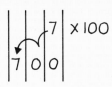

Multiply first by the six,
then by the hundred.

Multiplying by 100
helps us with this:

```
           147 r 4
    5 )  739
       -500 | 100 (5)
        239
       -200 |  40 (5)
         39
         35 |   7 (5)
          4 | 147 (5)
```

2 Copy and complete these:

a 4) 536 □
```
   -400 | □(4)
    136
   -□   | 30 (4)
     16
   -□   | □(4)
         □(4)
```

b 6) 893 □ r □
```
   -□ | 100 (6)
   293
   -□ |  40 (6)
   □
   -□ | □(6)
   □  | □(6)
```

c 3) 598 □ r □
```
   -□ | □(3)
   □
   -□ | □(3)
   □
   -□ | □(3)
   □  | □(3)
```

1 Do these the same way:

a 376 ÷ 2   **c** 671 ÷ 5   **e** 831 ÷ 7   **g** 975 ÷ 8

b 439 ÷ 3   **d** 624 ÷ 4   **f** 846 ÷ 6   **h** 981 ÷ 9

Sometimes multiples of 100 can be used. It shortens the working if they are.

```
              279 r 2
      3 )   839
          −600 | 200  (3)
           239
          −210 |  70  (3)
            29
          − 27 |   9  (3)
             2 | 279  (3)
```

2 Copy and complete these:

```
a  4 )   936
      − □ | □ (4)
        □
      − 120 | □ (4)
        □
      −  16 | □ (4)
            | □ (4)
```

```
b  2 )   947
      − 800 | □ (2)
        147
      −  □ | □ (2)
        □
      −  □ | □ (2)
        □ | □ (2)
```

```
c  3 )   834
      − □ | □ (3)
        □
      − □ | □ (3)
        □
      − □ | □ (3)
          | □ (3)
```

d 749 ÷ 3   **f** 826 ÷ 2   **h** 713 ÷ 2   **j** 874 ÷ 3

e 911 ÷ 4   **g** 630 ÷ 3   **i** 981 ÷ 4   **k** 999 ÷ 4

Dividing by numbers greater than 10

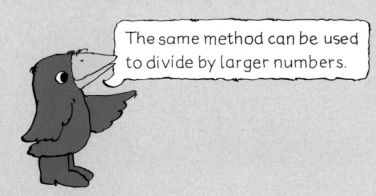

The same method can be used to divide by larger numbers.

```
              15 r 1
     13 )   196
          −130 | 10 (13)
            66
          − 65 |  5 (13)
             1 | 15 (13)
```

1   Copy and complete

a
$$
\begin{array}{r}
\boxed{}\,r\,\boxed{} \\
15\,)\,\overline{193} \\
\end{array}
$$
$-\boxed{}$ | 10 (15)
$\boxed{}$
$-\;30$ | $\boxed{}$ (15)
$\boxed{}$ | $\boxed{}$ (15)

b
$$
\begin{array}{r}
\boxed{}\,r\,\boxed{} \\
17\,)\,\overline{218} \\
\end{array}
$$
$-\boxed{}$ | 10 (17)
48
$-\boxed{}$ | $\boxed{}$ (17)
$\boxed{}$ | $\boxed{}$ (17)

c
$$
\begin{array}{r}
\boxed{}\,r\,\boxed{} \\
18\,)\,\overline{222} \\
\end{array}
$$
$-\boxed{}$ | $\boxed{}$ (18)
$\boxed{}$
$-\boxed{}$ | $\boxed{}$ (18)
$\boxed{}$ | $\boxed{}$ (18)

d $173 \div 14$
e $198 \div 16$

f $185 \div 15$
g $203 \div 17$

h $172 \div 13$
i $221 \div 19$

j $216 \div 18$
k $292 \div 17$

Sometimes multiples of 10 can be used. It shortens the working if they are.

$$
\begin{array}{r}
25\;r\;7 \\
17\,)\,\overline{432} \\
\end{array}
$$
-340 | 20 (17)
92
$-\;85$ | 5 (17)
7 | 25 (17)

2   Do these the same way:

a $312 \div 13$
b $477 \div 15$

c $321 \div 12$
d $414 \div 14$

e $765 \div 15$
f $552 \div 17$

g $816 \div 19$
h $937 \div 18$

3   a John has 408 stamps. He sticks them on 17 pages of his album.
      If there are the same number on each page, how many stamps are
      there on a page?

   b In a school 392 children are equally divided into 14 classes.
      How many are there in each class?

   c In the class library each shelf, on average, holds 18 books.
      How many shelves will be needed for 432 books?

   d Fifteen biscuits make one packet. How many packets can be made
      from 476 biscuits? How many are left?

   e How many perfume bottles, each holding 16 millilitres, can be filled
      from a $\frac{1}{2}$-litre container?

Chapter 19: Time

The 24-hour clock

The clock shows half-past eight or 8.30. To make sure people know if we mean morning or evening, we have to say a.m. (before noon) or p.m. (after noon). As there are 24 hours in a day, if we use the 24-hour system for telling the time we do not have to say a.m. or p.m.

8.30 a.m. is 08.30   8.30 p.m. is 20.30

Notice that each number on the inner ring (the p.m. part) is 12 more than the number in the outer ring.
6 a.m. is 06.00   but 6 p.m. is 18.00.
11.15 a.m. is 11.15 but 11.15 p.m. is 23.15.

1 Use a strip of squared paper to make a 'time line' like this:

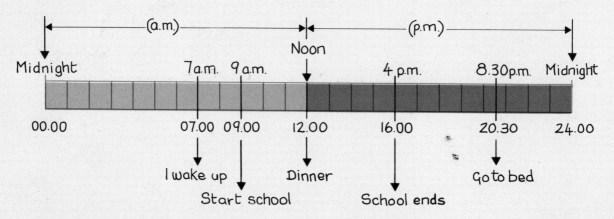

Mark in some special times of the day using both a.m./p.m. and 24-hour systems.

2 Write these times using the 24-hour system. Always use two figures for the hours (01, 02, 03, . . . 09, 10, 11, . . . 23, 24) and two figures for the minutes (00 . . . 59).

a 1 a.m.	**e** 5 p.m.	**i** 10.25 p.m.	**m** 1 minute to midnight
b 1 p.m.	**f** midnight	**j** 8.45 p.m.	**n** 1 minute past midnight
c noon	**g** 9.30 p.m.	**k** 2.35 p.m.	**o** 5 past noon
d 5 a.m.	**h** 10.15 a.m.	**l** 5 past 3 p.m.	**p** 10 to 3 p.m.

From one time to another

Working out how long from 9.15 a.m. to 4.25 p.m., for example,
is much easier using the 24-hour system.

Using the 12-hour system:

	h	min
from 9.15 a.m. to 10 a.m. is		45
from 10 a.m. to noon is	2	
from noon to 4.25 p.m. is	4	25
	6	70 = 7h 10min.

Using the 24-hour system

	h	min
	16	25
−	09	15
	7	10

from 09:15   to 16:25

1 Use the 24-hour system to find how long between times shown by
the two clock faces or digital displays:

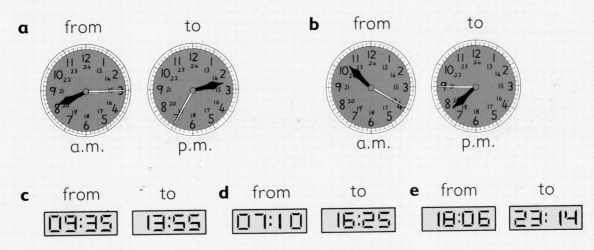

a from   to   **b** from   to

a.m.   p.m.   a.m.   p.m.

c from 09:35 to 13:55 **d** from 07:10 to 16:25 **e** from 18:06 to 23:14

2 **a** Anne starts school at 09.15 and finishes at 15.45.
How many hours and minutes is she at school?

b If she has $1\frac{1}{4}$ hours for dinner time and two play-times of 15 minutes
each, how much time is there for lessons?

3 **a** A marathon race started at 14.05 and the winner crossed the
finishing line at 19.53. How long did he take?

b The second runner came in 12 minutes later.
At what time did he finish?

Train, bus and airway timetables are printed in the 24-hour system.
They do not have to print a.m. or p.m. hundreds of times.

1 Work out the time taken for each of these journeys:

	depart	arrive		depart	arrive		depart	arrive
a	10.15 a.m.	5 p.m.	**d**	8.35 a.m.	9.10 a.m.	**g**	3.48 a.m.	13.40 p.m.
b	5.30 a.m.	noon	**e**	8.35 a.m.	9.10 p.m.	**h**	5.55 p.m.	9.12 p.m.
c	11.45 a.m.	9.15 p.m.	**f**	6.50 a.m.	1.15 p.m.	**i**	7.32 a.m.	5.10 p.m.

If there are 'not enough' minutes for
a subtraction, exchange
1 hour for 60 minutes.
16.20 becomes 15h and 80mins.

$$
\begin{array}{r}
15.80 \\
\cancel{16.20} \\
-11.50 \\
\hline
4.30
\end{array}
$$

2 Change these times to the 24-hour system and find the time taken for
each journey:

	depart	arrive		depart	arrive		depart	arrive
a	11.00	15.00	**d**	01.00	18.00	**g**	14.15	19.28
b	08.00	09.30	**e**	05.00	14.30	**h**	09.32	13.48
c	16.00	23.00	**f**	06.30	12.45	**i**	07.10	07.37

Sometimes the full stop
between hours and
minutes is missed out,
so that a railway
timetable looks
like this:

Exeter Central	0639	0758	1352	1642	2253
Topsham	0651	0815	1404	1655	2305
Exton	0655	0819	1408	1659	2309
Commando Camp	0657	0821	1410	1701	2311
Exmouth	0704	0828	1417	1708	2318

3 a Do the trains all take the same time over each part of the journey?
  b List the time taken from each station to the next by the 2253 train
    from Exeter Central.
  c At what time does the slowest train leave Exeter Central?
  d If you arrive at Topsham at half-past three in the afternoon,
    how long will you have to wait for the next train to Exmouth?
  e What is the time of the latest train you can catch from Exeter
    Central to be sure of getting to Exmouth by 6 p.m.?

4 Make a timetable of your own for journeys from Exmouth to Exeter
Central.

Multiplication of time

John's father works 7 hours 15 minutes a day.
How many hours and minutes does he work in a 5-day week?

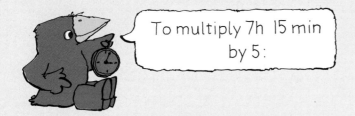

Set out the hours and minutes in
separate columns like this:

Multiply the 15 min by 5 and write
the answer, 75 mins, below the answer line.

75 min = (60 min + 15 min) = 1h 15 min

Write 15 in the minutes column and
the small 1 under the hours column.

7h × 5 = 35h. Add on the 1h to make 36h.

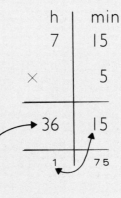

1 Set these out in the same way:
   a 2h 25 min × 3   d 3h 10 min × 9   g 8h 45 min × 7
   b 4h 15 min × 4   e 6h 12 min × 5   h 4h 52 min × 4
   c 8h 5 min × 8   f 7h 22 min × 6   i 9h 58 min × 8

2 A school's heating is switched on at 08.30 and switched off at 15.10
   each day.
   a How long is the heating on each day?
   b How long is the heating on in a 5-day week?

3 A nurse is on duty from 12.10 to 20.00 each day for 6 days.
   How many hours is this?

4 The night-duty nurse starts at 20.00 and comes off duty at 06.15
   the next day.
   a How long is this?
   b How many hours duty will a night nurse do in 6 nights?

Chapter 20: Fractions 2

Along the top this number line shows 0, 1 and 2. Below the line it is marked in eighths. Point A can be described in two ways —at the top it is $1\frac{3}{8}$ and at the bottom $\frac{11}{8}$.

1 Describe points B, C, D, E in the same way.

Numbers which are whole numbers and fractions, like $1\frac{3}{8}$ and $2\frac{1}{8}$ are **mixed numbers**.

Numbers which have larger numerators than denominators like $\frac{11}{8}$ and $\frac{19}{8}$ are **improper fractions**.

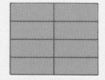 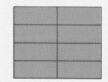 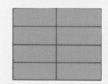 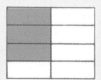

2 This diagram shows the mixed number $3\frac{3}{8}$.
Each whole one is $\frac{8}{8}$ so altogether $3(\frac{8}{8})+\frac{3}{8}=\frac{24}{8}+\frac{3}{8}=\frac{27}{8}$

Copy and complete :

a $1\frac{4}{5}=\frac{\square}{5}$ **d** $3\frac{1}{4}=\frac{\square}{4}$ **g** $3\frac{4}{5}=\frac{\square}{5}$ **j** $4\frac{7}{8}=\frac{\square}{8}$

b $2\frac{2}{3}=\frac{\square}{3}$ **e** $3\frac{2}{3}=\frac{\square}{3}$ **h** $4\frac{1}{4}=\frac{\square}{4}$ **k** $5\frac{7}{10}=\frac{\square}{10}$

c $2\frac{4}{5}=\frac{\square}{5}$ **f** $2\frac{7}{8}=\frac{\square}{8}$ **i** $4\frac{2}{3}=\frac{\square}{3}$ **l** $6\frac{2}{3}=\frac{\square}{3}$

Change $\frac{11}{4}$ to a mixed number. Each whole number will be $\frac{4}{4}$ so $\frac{11}{4}=2\frac{3}{4}$.

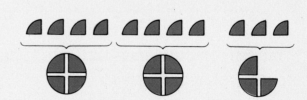

3 Change to mixed numbers :

a $\frac{7}{2}$ **d** $\frac{19}{4}$ **g** $\frac{27}{8}$ **j** $\frac{64}{9}$

b $\frac{14}{3}$ **e** $\frac{27}{5}$ **h** $\frac{41}{10}$ **k** $\frac{55}{8}$

c $\frac{13}{5}$ **f** $\frac{25}{6}$ **i** $\frac{43}{8}$ **l** $\frac{76}{9}$

Addition of mixed numbers

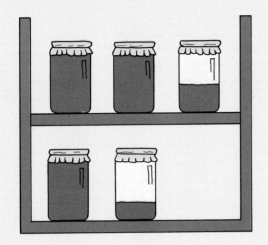

If there are $2\frac{1}{2}$ jars of jam on the top shelf and $1\frac{1}{3}$ jars on the bottom shelf, how much jam is there altogether?

	$2\frac{1}{2}+1\frac{1}{3}$
(There are 3 full jars.)	$3+\frac{1}{2}+\frac{1}{3}$
(change $\frac{1}{2}$ and $\frac{1}{3}$ into sixths.)	$3+\frac{3}{6}+\frac{2}{6}$
	$3\frac{5}{6}$

1 Do these in the same way:

a $3\frac{1}{4}+1\frac{1}{3}$ **c** $4\frac{2}{5}+1\frac{1}{3}$ **e** $3\frac{2}{3}+4\frac{1}{8}$ **g** $2\frac{2}{3}+3\frac{1}{8}$

b $2\frac{1}{2}+3\frac{3}{10}$ **d** $3\frac{2}{5}+1\frac{1}{4}$ **f** $2\frac{3}{10}+3\frac{1}{4}$ **h** $4\frac{1}{6}+2\frac{3}{4}$

Add $4\frac{2}{3}+3\frac{3}{5} = 7+\frac{10}{15}+\frac{9}{15}$

$\qquad = 7\frac{19}{15}$

$\qquad = 7+1\frac{4}{15}$

$\qquad = 8\frac{4}{15}$

This is an improper fraction and $\frac{19}{15} = 1\frac{4}{15}$

2 Do these in the same way:

a $2\frac{2}{3}+3\frac{3}{4}$ **d** $4\frac{3}{4}+2\frac{2}{5}$ **g** $3\frac{2}{3}+2\frac{4}{5}$ **j** $2\frac{7}{8}+4\frac{3}{5}$

b $1\frac{1}{2}+3\frac{3}{5}$ **e** $1\frac{3}{8}+4\frac{2}{3}$ **h** $2\frac{3}{4}+5\frac{7}{12}$ **k** $3\frac{7}{9}+3\frac{1}{4}$

c $2\frac{3}{8}+1\frac{2}{3}$ **f** $5\frac{7}{10}+3\frac{3}{4}$ **i** $1\frac{5}{8}+4\frac{2}{3}$ **l** $4\frac{5}{8}+5\frac{7}{10}$

Subtraction of mixed numbers

If there are $3\frac{1}{2}$ cakes on the table how can we take $1\frac{2}{3}$ away?

$3\frac{1}{2} - 1\frac{2}{3}$

I can take 1 away.

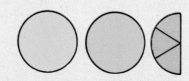

$2\frac{1}{2} - \frac{2}{3}$

Change $\frac{1}{2}$ and $\frac{2}{3}$ into sixths.

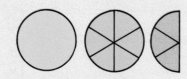

$= 2\frac{3}{6} - \frac{4}{6}$

There are not enough sixths to take $\frac{4}{6}$ away so I must change one of my whole ones into sixths.

$= 1\frac{9}{6} - \frac{4}{6}$

$= 1\frac{5}{6}$

1 Do these in the same way:

a $3\frac{1}{2} - 1\frac{3}{4}$ **d** $4\frac{1}{5} - 2\frac{1}{4}$ **g** $5\frac{1}{2} - 3\frac{3}{5}$ **j** $6\frac{4}{9} - 5\frac{1}{2}$

b $4\frac{1}{3} - 2\frac{1}{2}$ **e** $4\frac{2}{3} - 1\frac{4}{5}$ **h** $6\frac{1}{2} - 4\frac{5}{6}$ **k** $4\frac{5}{9} - 2\frac{3}{4}$

c $5\frac{2}{3} - 3\frac{7}{8}$ **f** $6\frac{3}{8} - 4\frac{2}{3}$ **i** $5\frac{2}{5} - 1\frac{2}{3}$ **l** $4\frac{2}{3} - 3\frac{7}{8}$

Chapter 21: Length 2

Measuring in millimetres

This ruler, marked in millimetres (mm) is used to measure the length of a paper clip.

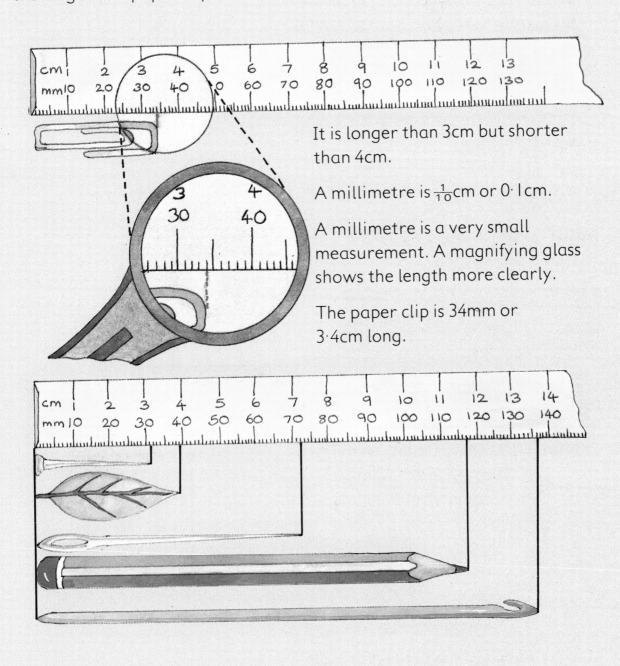

It is longer than 3cm but shorter than 4cm.

A millimetre is $\frac{1}{10}$cm or 0·1cm.

A millimetre is a very small measurement. A magnifying glass shows the length more clearly.

The paper clip is 34mm or 3·4cm long.

I Record the length first in millimetres then in centimetres of:

a the pin   **c** the needle   **e** the crochet hook

b the leaf   **d** the pencil

Remember: there are 10 millimetres (mm) in 1 centimetre (cm)
so 1mm = $\frac{1}{10}$cm = 0·1cm.

1
a ☐ mm = 2cm   **e** 80mm = ☐ cm   **i** ☐ mm = 9·2cm
b ☐ mm = 7cm   **f** 85mm = ☐ cm   **j** ☐ mm = 0·1cm
c ☐ mm = 0·7cm   **g** 3mm = ☐ cm   **k** 120mm = ☐ cm
d 30mm = ☐ cm   **h** 100mm = ☐ cm   **l** 135mm = ☐ cm

10 millimetres = 1 centimetre
100 centimetres = 1 metre
   1 000 millimetres = 1 metre

'milli' comes from a Latin word
meaning a 'thousand'.

1mm = $\frac{1}{1000}$m = 0·001m

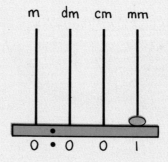

285mm = 200mm + 80mm + 5mm
     = 20cm + 8cm + 5mm
     = 2dm + 8cm + 5mm
     = 0·2m + 0·08m + 0·005m
     = 0·285m

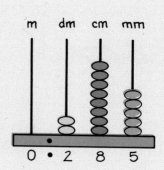

2 Draw abacus pictures of these measurements and record them
in metres:

a 346mm   **c** 307mm   **e** 80mm   **g** 990mm   **i** 1234mm
b 520mm   **d** 25mm   **f** 6mm   **h** 1000mm   **j** 1050mm

1 a Use a ruler marked in mm to check these measurements.
Make sure the zero is level with the end of the line.

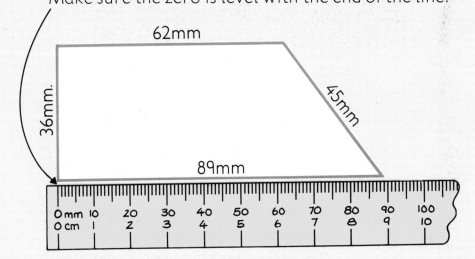

b Estimate the perimeter of this shape
c Work out the perimeter and record it first in mm then in m.

2 Measure the sides of these shapes in millimetres.
Estimate and then work out the perimeter of each shape.
Record in mm and m.

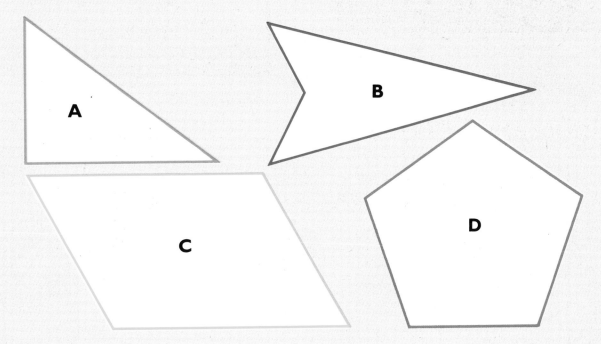

3 a Write down the names of the shapes in question 2.
b What is the difference between the longest and shortest perimeters?
c What is the quicker way of working out the perimeter of **D**?

To find the perimeter of
a regular octagon with sides
129mm long, multiply 129mm × 8.
(Estimate first:
129mm × 8 ≃ 130mm × 8 = 1040mm)
Perimeter is 1032mm or 1·032 metres.

```
    129
  ×   8
     72 (   9 × 8)
    160 (  20 × 8)
    800 (100 × 8)
   1032
```

or

```
    129
  ×   8
   1032
     27
```

1   If a regular octagon has a perimeter of 1 metre,
    what is the length of a side in mm?

2   Estimate and then work out the perimeter of a regular
    hexagon whose sides are 172mm long.

This graph paper is marked in
centimetre and 2-millimetre squares.
The side of each small square
is 2mm long.

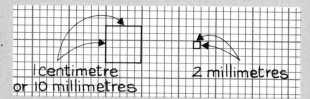

3   Spread out your hand first on a strip of graph paper. Carefully mark
    where the tips of your thumb and little finger come and measure your
    hand-span as accurately as you can in millimetres. Measure
    the hand-span in mm of some of your friends and draw a graph of them.

4   Is your left hand-span the same as your right hand-span?

5   Use 2-mm graph paper to measure accurately the diameters of different
    coins (10p, 5p, 2p, 1p, $\frac{1}{2}$p), the length and breadth of stamps and the
    lengths of screws, bolts, nails, etc.

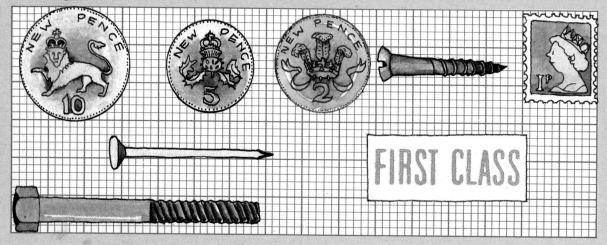

Chapter 1: Place Value 1

G_____g in f___s: addition

We have met Mr Sweet who makes
choc-bars in his factory.
He packs 5 bars into a box.

Mr Sweet went to the store to see how many choc-bars he had.

On the top shelf were
2 boxes and 2 bars
and on the bottom shelf
1 box and 4 bars.

But 6 bars are
1 box and 1 bar.

So he has:

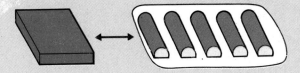

boxes	bars
2	2
+ 1	4
3	- 6
4	1

If we use base 5 longs and units, we can do some more problems.

1 unit stands for 1 choc-bar.
1 long stands for 1 box.

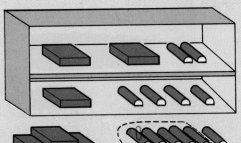

1 box 4 bars			▶		
1 box 2 bars					
2 boxes 6 bars			▶		
3 boxes 1 bar			▶		

1 Set out base 5 longs and units and work out these:

a boxes bars	**b** boxes bars	**c** boxes bars	**d** boxes bars
2 0	1 3	4	1 .4
+ 1 3	+ 2 3	+ 1 2	+ 1 4

Grouping in sixes: addition

Mrs Giles packs eggs in boxes.
Each box holds 6 eggs.

On Sunday the hens
laid 8 eggs.
Mrs Giles put 6 into
a box so that she had
I box and 2 eggs.——→

On Monday the hens
laid 5 eggs. ——→

But she can put
6 eggs in
another box.
So she has: ——→

	boxes	eggs
	I	2
	+	5
	I	7
	2	I

This time we can use base 6 longs and units.

I unit to stand for I egg.

I long stands for I box.

Set out base 6 longs and units (or cubes which fit together to make
sticks of 6) and work out these:

I

a
boxes	eggs
I	3
+	5

c
boxes	eggs
2	4
+ I	3

e
boxes	eggs
I	0
+	5

g
boxes	eggs
2	I
+ 2	5

b
boxes	eggs
2	5
+ I	5

d
boxes	eggs
I	4
+ 3	4

f
boxes	eggs
I	2
+ I	4

h
boxes	eggs
I	5
+	5

Using the multi-base board for addition

John is using squares, longs and units in the base four set.

A long is made from 4 units.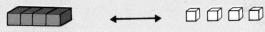

A square is made from 4 longs.

He sets out these on the multi-base board.

He records:

squares	longs	units		S	L	U
				1	2	3
He adds 2 more units.				+		2
He puts them together.						
He makes another long. This is the answer:				1	3	1

This time he sets up:

He records:

squares	longs	units		S	L	U
				1	3	1
He adds 1 long and 2 units.				+	1	2
He puts them together.						
Now he can make another square.				2	0	3

The zero means there are no longs.

1 Use a multi-base board with squares, longs and units (base 4) to do these:

a
```
  S L U
  1 2 3
+     3
```

b
```
  S L U
  2 1 2
+   1 3
```

c
```
  S L U
  1 3 1
+ 1 1 1
```

d
```
  S L U
  1 0 3
+   1 1
```

In base five

A long is made from 5 units.

A square is made from 5 longs.

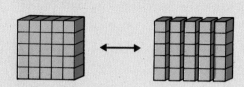

1 Use a multi-base board, squares, longs and units (base 5) for these:

a	S	L	U
	1	1	2
+		1	4

b	S	L	U
	1	2	2
+		4	1

c	S	L	U
	2	2	3
+		1	3

d	S	L	U
	2	1	4
+		4	2

In base ten

A long is made from 10 units.

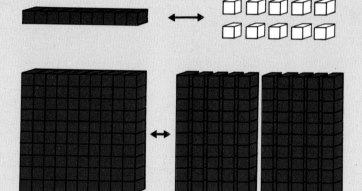

A square is made from 10 longs.

2 Use a multi-base board, squares, longs and units for these:

a	S	L	U
	1	2	3
+		4	1

b	S	L	U
		3	6
+		1	5

c	S	L	U
		4	2
+		7	3

d	S	L	U
		3	0
+		8	2

e	S	L	U
	1	6	2
+		1	9

f	S	L	U
		4	3	6
+	1	7	3

g	S	L	U
		3	2
+		6	8

h	S	L	U
	2	9	9
+	1	0	4

The abacus

An early abacus was made by placing pebbles in grooves. When the 'units' groove held ten pebbles, they were removed and one pebble was put in the 'tens' groove.

2 7

This abacus shows 2 tens and 7 units or 27.

Here is an abacus made from beads threaded onto wires.

The beads on this wire show how many units.

The beads on this wire show how many tens.

2 tens 1 unit

We can record any number on an abacus. (For large numbers we would need more wires.) Read these abacus numbers.

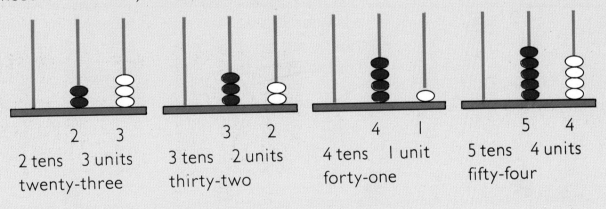

2   3
2 tens 3 units
twenty-three

3   2
3 tens 2 units
thirty-two

4   1
4 tens 1 unit
forty-one

5   4
5 tens 4 units
fifty-four

1 Copy these abacus pictures into your book and write the number they show.

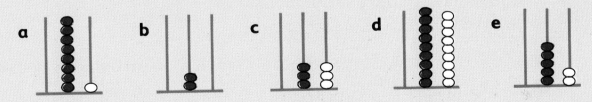

a   b   c   d   e

2 Draw abacus pictures for these numbers:

a sixty-four   c eighty   e ninety-nine   g 7 tens and 3 units
b 50   d five   f five tens   h four tens and 2 units

A dash called a **hyphen** is used to join some number words.

For example,
43 forty-three
78 seventy-eight

I Write these in words.

The words in the box will help you.

a 57 **e** 42
b 29 **f** 75
c 36 **g** 38
d 31 **h** 64

twenty	one
thirty	two
forty	three
fifty	four
sixty	five
seventy	six
eighty	seven
ninety	eight
	nine

Addition on the abacus

For example: 13 + 2 = 15

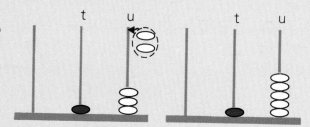

27 + 5

This column is full so we exchange ten beads for one and put it on the tens.

Now put on the other two units to make:

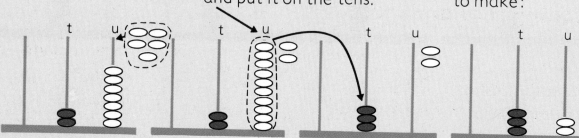

2 Use your abacus to do these additions.
Draw an abacus picture of each answer.

a 17 + 2   **e** 49 + 1   **i** 38 + 2 tens   **m** sixteen + twelve
b 22 + 6   **f** 35 + 10   **j** 52 + 17   **n** 69 + 1
c 24 + 10   **g** forty-four + 7   **k** seven + twelve   **o** 40 + 40
d 19 + 2   **h** 45 + 1 ten   **l** seventy + twelve   **p** eighteen + 13

3 Add 10 to each of these numbers: 5, 9, 20, 12, 23, 90.

Chapter 2: Addition 1

Adding tens

The abacus shows 3 tens. 2 more tens are put on 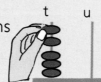 to make 5 tens or fifty.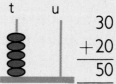

$$\begin{array}{r} 30 \\ +20 \\ \hline 50 \end{array}$$

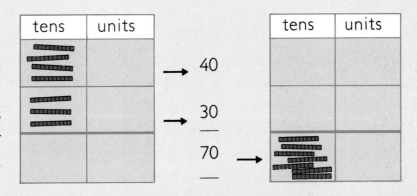

The counting board shows:
4 tens → 40

and 3 tens added together to give 7 tens. → 30

70 →

1 Copy and complete. Use an abacus or counting board.
a 50+20 =   **c** 7 tens+20 =   **e** 10+40+20+10 =
b 30+60 =   **d** 30+2 tens =   **f** 2 tens+40+3 tens =

Adding tens and units

Follow the pictures to see how the counting board is used to add 32 and 25.

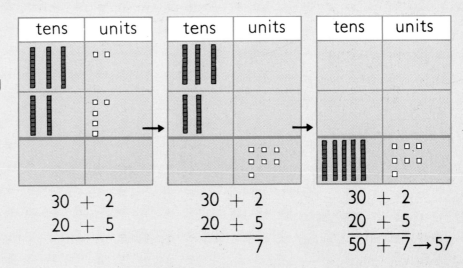

$$\begin{array}{r} 30 + 2 \\ 20 + 5 \\ \hline \end{array}$$

$$\begin{array}{r} 30 + 2 \\ 20 + 5 \\ \hline 7 \end{array}$$

$$\begin{array}{r} 30 + 2 \\ 20 + 5 \\ \hline 50 + 7 \rightarrow 57 \end{array}$$

2 Do these the same way:

a 43 +22   **b** 57 +12   **c** 61 +25   **d** 20 +69   **e** 54 +42   **f** 47 +41   **g** 63 +36

Use the counting
board for 27+15.

tens	units
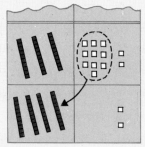	

Set out 27 as 20+7 ⟶

and 15 as 10+5 ⟶

Add them together:

3 tens and 12 units   30+12

Exchange 10 units for I ten-rod
and put it in the tens column.
30+10+2

4 tens and 2 units ⟶ 42

I Do these in the
same way.

a	54	**e**	75
	+27		+18
b	56	**f**	69
	+38		+21
c	63	**g**	46
	+29		+37
d	45	**h**	83
	+37		+ 9

2   Try these **without** using rods or the abacus. Copy and complete:

a   36 ⟶ ☐ +6
  +25 ⟶ 20+☐
    50+11 ⟶ 50+☐ +☐ ⟶ 61

b   47 ⟶ ☐ +☐
  +26 ⟶ ☐ +☐
    60 +☐ ⟶ 60+☐ + 3 ⟶ ☐

Use the same method for these:

c	44	**d**	66	**e**	46	**f**	33	**g**	65	**h**	52
	+18		+28		+46		+27		+26		+38

Here is another
way to set out
your work.

28
+47
―――
15 (8+7)
60 (20+40)
―――
75

3   Copy and complete:

a   46
  +38
  ―――
  14 (☐+8)
  70 (40+☐)
  ―――
  84

b   65
  +26
  ―――
  ☐ (5+6)
  ☐ (60+20)
  ―――
  ☐

c	74	**d**	57	**e**	48	**f**	51	**g**	66	**h**	58
	+18		+36		+19		+39		+28		+27

An even shorter way of
recording what happens
on the counting board is:

8+7 = 15; put the 5 units in
the answer.
Record the 'ten' below the line
in the tens column.
Add the tens; 20+10 = 30 and
I ten below the line makes 4 tens.

```
  28
+ 17
----
  45
   1
```

> Don't forget
> the ten under
> the tens column.

1 Use the shorter method for these:

a 67
+25

c 39
+29

e 48
+37

g 56
+ 9

i 75
+15

k 23
+55

b 76
+17

d 16
+24

f 38
+29

h 44
+25

j 64
+29

l 38
+32

Sometimes there may be more than two numbers
to add together.
Use the same way as before but be extra careful.
Always check your answer.

```
  42
+26
 17
 85
  1
```

2 Now try these:

a 44
+33
16

b 56
+25
18

c 48
+20
24

d 46
+28
17

e 69
+ 9
20

f 28
+26
25
17

Sometimes you may have to put the figures in
columns yourself. For example: Add these numbers.

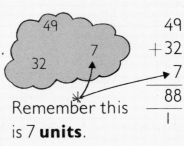

49
32
7

```
  49
+32
  7
 88
  1
```

Remember this
is 7 **units**.

In addition, the answer is called
the **sum** or **total**.

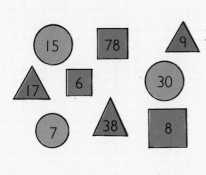

15 78 9
17 6   30
7   38 8

3 Find the total of the numbers:

a in the squares,
b in the triangles,
c in the circles.
d What is the grand total of all the numbers?

Try these addition problems.
The first one is set out for you.

$$\begin{array}{r} 13 \\ +33 \\ 3 \\ \hline \\ \hline \end{array}$$

Set the problems out like this.

1 a Add thirteen, thirty-three and three.

b Find the sum of fourteen, four and forty-four.

c Add twenty-five, thirty-five and fifteen.

d What is the total when twenty-one, seventeen and nineteen are added?

e Eighteen plus twenty-seven plus thirty-one gives what total?

f Mary spent 37 pence at the grocer's, 25 pence at the sweet shop and 28 pence at the baker's. How much did she spend altogether?

g Peter has collected 49 British stamps, 24 French stamps and 8 German. What is his total number of stamps?

h Mrs Giles collected 17 eggs on Monday, 8 on Tuesday, 11 on Wednesday and 19 on Thursday. How many eggs did she collect altogether?

Magic squares

16	9	14
11	13	15
12	17	10

2 Add the numbers in each row.
Add the numbers in each column.
Add the numbers in each diagonal.

3 Add 7 to the number in each cell to make a new magic square. Draw it in your book. What is the new total for each row, column and diagonal? Try adding other numbers to each cell.

4 Check that this is a magic square.

16	2	3	13
5	11	10	8
9	7	6	12
4	14	15	1

5 Work out and write in your book the numbers missing in this magic square.

14	9	13	
	11	7	16
3	12	8	15
17	6	10	5

Chapter 3: Shape 1

Turning

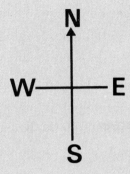

If I stand facing North and turn through one complete turn, I shall be facing North again.

If I start by facing North and turn through half a complete turn, I shall be facing South.

If I start by facing North and turn to my right through a quarter of a turn, I shall be facing East.

If I start by facing North and turn to my left through a quarter of a complete turn, I shall be facing West.

I   Copy and complete.

I start facing:	I turn through:	direction	I finish facing:
South	A complete turn		
East	$\frac{1}{2}$ a complete turn		
West	$\frac{1}{4}$ of a complete turn	right	
South	$\frac{1}{4}$ of a complete turn	left	
West	A complete turn		
South	$\frac{1}{2}$ of a complete turn		
East	$\frac{1}{4}$ of a complete turn	right	
West	$\frac{1}{4}$ of a complete turn	left	
East	A complete turn		
West	$\frac{1}{2}$ of a complete turn		
South	$\frac{3}{4}$ of a complete turn	right	
East	$\frac{3}{4}$ of a complete turn	left	

Fold a circle of paper or thin card into four. Open it out and mark in the points.

As a pointer push a pipecleaner or straw up through the centre. (Bend it over at the back.)

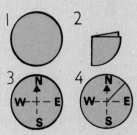

Use the pointer to check your answers to question 1.

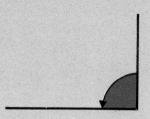

One quarter of a complete turn has a special name – a **right angle**. It is called a right angle because it is a true angle which makes a square corner.

1 Take a piece of paper, any shape, and fold it roughly in half. Now fold it in half again.

fold

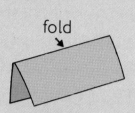

The corner where the folds meet is a **right angle**.

right angle

2 Use your right angle to find things in your classroom which have right angles for their corners. Make a list.

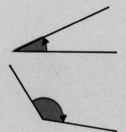

A turn which is less than a right angle is called an **acute angle**.

A turn which is more than one right angle but less than two right angles is called an **obtuse angle**.

3 Use your folded right angle to complete the sentences. The first is done for you.

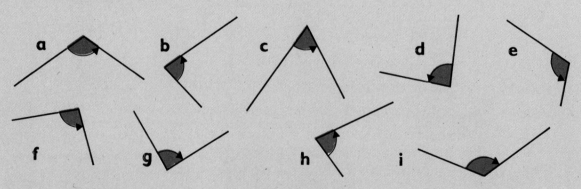

Angle **a** is obtuse.
Angle **b** is ☐
Angle **c** is ☐

Angle **d** is ☐
Angle **e** is ☐
Angle **f** is ☐

Angle **g** is ☐
Angle **h** is ☐
Angle **i** is ☐

Vertical and horizontal

Crooked houses are fun to visit
but not such fun to live in.

Can you see what is wrong with
this house?

Builders must make sure that the walls
are upright or **vertical**
and level or **horizontal**.

To make sure the walls are **vertical**
the builder uses a **plumb line**.

To make sure that they are
horizontal he uses a **spirit level**.

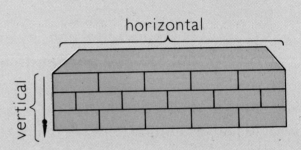

1   Make a plumb line from a piece of string with a small heavy weight
    at the end. Hold your plumb line by the side of the wall or door.
    Are the wall and the frame of the door vertical?
    Find some other verticals in the classroom.

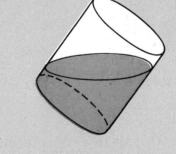

No matter how you tilt a container with
water in it, the surface of the water remains
level or horizontal. Can you discover where
the word horizontal comes from?

2   Make a simple spirit level by filling a bottle with water except
    for one bubble of air. Put on the top and lay it down flat.
    If the surface is horizontal the bubble will go to the centre
    of the bottle.

Use your spirit level to test some of the surfaces in
your classroom to see if they are horizontal.

1 Partly fill a jar with water and hold your plumb line in front of the jar.
Look at the water level.

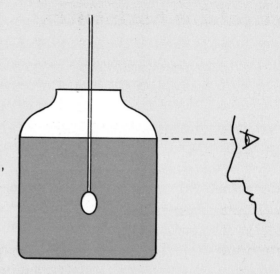

Can you say what angles you see, where your vertical line crosses your horizontal line?
Use your folded right angle to measure them.

Vertical and horizontal lines meet or cross at right angles.
We say that they are **perpendicular** to one another.

2 John was asked by his teacher to run and touch the wall as quickly as he could.

Which path did he take?
Why?

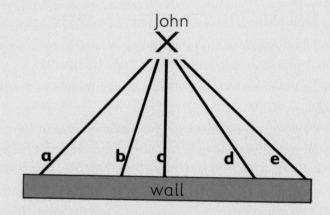

Copy this sentence putting in the missing word.

John's path and the wall are[   ] to each other.

3 Copy and complete the sentence.

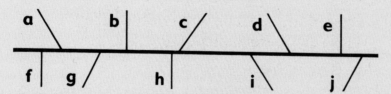

In the diagram, the lines perpendicular to the thick line are [   ]

4 Draw a line 8 cm long and draw four lines which are perpendicular to it.

Chapter 4: Length 1

Parts of a metre

You need:
a metre stick,
2 strips of paper
50cm long,
and I strip
10cm long.

Remember:
cm means centimetre
or centimetres.
m means metre or metres.

I Copy and complete.
   a There are ☐ 50cm strips in I metre.
   b Each 50 cm strip is ☐ a metre.
   c There are ☐ 10cm strips in I metre.
   d There are ☐ 10cm strips in ½ metre.

Now cut one of your 50cm strips in half.

2 Copy and complete.
   a Each half of the 50cm strip is about ☐ cm long.
   b There are ☐ 25cm strips in I metre.
   c Each one is a ☐qu _ _ _ _ of a metre.

3 Copy and complete. The first one is done for you.
   a 5 lots of 10cm = $\frac{1}{2}$m or 50 cm   e 1m − $\frac{1}{4}$m = △m or ☐ cm
   b $\frac{1}{2}$m − 25cm = △m or ☐ cm   f $\frac{1}{4}$m + $\frac{1}{4}$m + 10cm = ☐ cm
   c 50cm − $\frac{1}{4}$m = △m or ☐ cm   g $\frac{1}{2}$m − 10cm = ☐ cm
   d $\frac{1}{2}$m + $\frac{1}{4}$m + $\frac{1}{4}$m = △m or ☐ cm   h 1m − 10cm = ☐ cm

4 Use your 50cm, 25cm and 10cm strips to measure objects in your classroom. Make a list of at least 3 objects in each column.

Record like this:

Less than 10cm	10cm to 25cm	25cm to 50cm	50cm to 1m
rubber	book	desk	blackboard

The snail race

Three snails, Ali, Bess and Con, started
at the same time to crawl along a path.
The picture shows how far they had
gone after 1 hour.

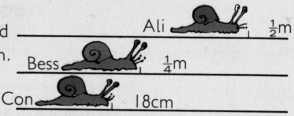

Ali $\frac{1}{2}$m

Bess $\frac{1}{4}$m

Con 18cm

1 Copy and complete:

In one hour: **a** Ali crawled ☐ cm farther than Bess.

b Bess went ☐ cm farther than Con.

c Ali went ☐ cm farther than Con.

d [   ] crawled the farthest.

e [   ] crawled the shortest distance.

f The fastest snail was [   ]

g The slowest snail was [   ]

The perimeter

Put your finger on the start
and follow the arrows.
The distance all around the shape
is called the perimeter.
The perimeter of this shape is 14cm.

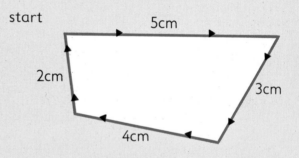

start

5cm

2cm

3cm

4cm

2 Work out the perimeters of these shapes:

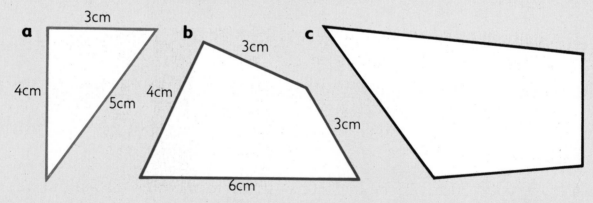

a
3cm
4cm
5cm

b
3cm
4cm
6cm

c
3cm

3 Use your ruler to find the perimeter of some objects in your classroom.
Record like this:

object	lengths of the sides	perimeter
book	15cm + 20cm + 15cm + 20cm	70cm

The decimetre (10cm) strip

Carefully measure and cut out a strip of card 10cm long.

10 cm

Check that the strip fits 10 times along the metre rule.
This means the strip is one tenth of a metre long.
It is a decimetre strip ("deci" means "tenth").

$$10 \, cm = 1 \text{ decimetre (dm)} = \tfrac{1}{10} \text{ metre}$$

1 Copy and complete:
   a 1 decimetre = ☐ cm
   b 2 decimetres = ☐ cm
   c 4 decimetres = ☐ cm
   d 5 decimetres = ☐ cm
   e 6dm   = ☐ cm
   f 7dm   = ☐ cm
   g 9dm   = ☐ cm
   h 10dm   = ☐ cm

Carefully mark off your decimetre strip into centimetres.

| 1 | 2 | 3 | 4 | 5 | 6 | 7 | 8 | 9 | 10 |

2 The length of this pencil is 1dm strip and 4cm 'left over'.

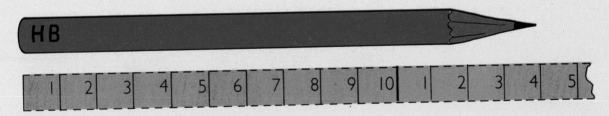

HB

| 1 | 2 | 3 | 4 | 5 | 6 | 7 | 8 | 9 | 10 | 1 | 2 | 3 | 4 | 5 |

Use your decimetre strip to measure objects in the classroom.
Record like this:

object	number of dm strips	cm "left over"	total measurement
pencil	1	4	14cm
width of this book	2	1	21cm

Chapter 5: Addition 2

Introducing the hundred

I is added to
99 to make 100.

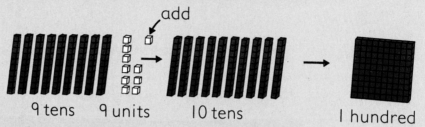

9 tens   9 units   10 tens   I hundred

On an abacus, 99 is recorded like this:

If I unit is added, there are ten units. add I

The 10 units are exchanged for I ten to make 10

The 10 tens are exchanged for I hundred.

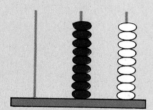 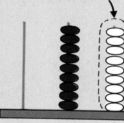 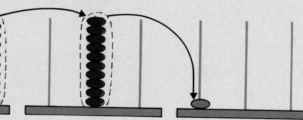

Two hundred and thirty-six can be written as 236. It looks like this in squares, longs and units.

hundreds	tens	units

It can be recorded like this on an abacus.

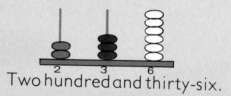

2   3   6
Two hundred and thirty-six.

I Here are some numbers set out in squares, longs and units.
Draw an abacus picture.
Write the numbers in figures and words.

a

hundreds	tens	units

b

hundreds	tens	units

c

hundreds	tens	units

d

hundreds	tens	units

e

hundreds	tens	units

1 Copy these abacus pictures and write the number they show in words and figures.

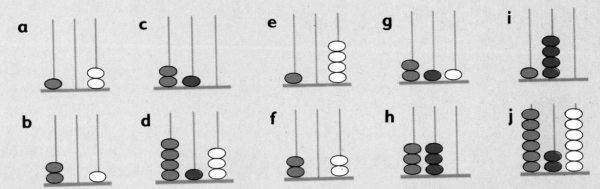

a   c   e   g   i

b   d   f   h   j

2 Draw abacus pictures for these and write the numbers in figures underneath.
   a Two hundred and nineteen   e Three hundred and seventy
   b One hundred and five   f Seven hundred and one
   c Eighty-seven   g One hundred and thirty
   d Two hundred and twenty-four   h Two hundred and twelve

3 Add 1 to each of these numbers.
Draw an abacus picture of your answer, and write it in words and figures.
For example: 211+1

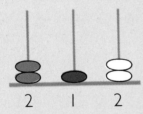

2   1   2

two hundred and twelve

a	100	e	234	i	109
b	103	f	310	j	209
c	120	g	99	k	229
d	219	h	409	l	499

4 Add 10 to each of these numbers.
Draw an abacus picture of your answer, and write it in words and figures.
For example: 105+10

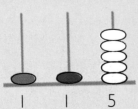

1   1   5

One hundred and fifteen

a	201	e	890	i	301
b	7	f	299	j	96
c	111	g	219	k	509
d	57	h	394	l	90

Adding hundreds, tens and units

Follow the picture diagrams to see how the
counting board can be used to add 254 and 169.

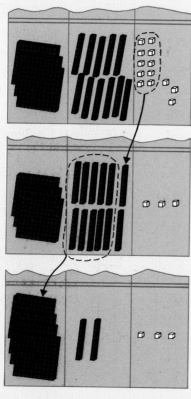

hundreds	tens	units

Set out 254

$$200 + 50 + 4$$

and 169

$$100 + 60 + 9$$

Add them together.

Exchange 10 units for
1 ten rod.

Exchange 10 ten rods for
1 hundred square.

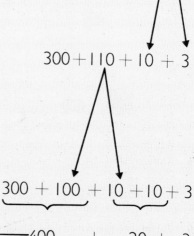

$$300 + 110 + 13$$

$$300 + 110 + 10 + 3$$

$$300 + 100 + 10 + 10 + 3$$

423 ◄—————————— 400 + 20 + 3

I Use some squares, longs and units on a counting board to do these.

a 256	**b** 374	**c** 287	**d** 463	**e** 256
+128	+163	+184	+177	+447

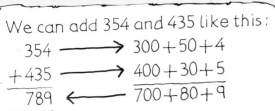

We can add 354 and 435 like this:

$$354 \longrightarrow 300+50+4$$
$$+435 \longrightarrow 400+30+5$$
$$789 \longleftarrow 700+80+9$$

Now look at this:

$$258 \longrightarrow 200 + 50 + 8$$
$$+179 \longrightarrow 100 + 70 + 9$$
$$300 + 120 + 17$$

$$300 + 100 + 20 + 10 + 7$$

$$437 \longleftarrow 400 + 30 + 7$$

Here is another way to set out your work:

$$
\begin{array}{r}
378 \\
+149 \\
\hline
17 \quad (8+9) \\
110 \quad (70+40) \\
400 \quad (300+100) \\
\hline
527 \\
\end{array}
$$

1 Set these out in the same way.

a 253
  +145

c 172
  +206

e 348
  +151

b 505
  +272

d 316
  + 82

f 147
  +741

2 Set these out in the same way.

a 575
  +319

c 493
  +472

e 708
  +199

b 428
  +315

d 254
  + 89

f 675
  +146

3 Set these out like the example.

a 675
  +279

c 765
  +295

e 829
  +198

b 706
  +284

d 438
  +362

f 497
  +303

There is an even shorter way of recording addition.

$$
\begin{array}{r}
378 \\
+149 \\
\hline
527 \\
\hline
1\ 1 \\
\end{array}
$$

$8+9 =17.$ Put the 7 units in the answer.

Record the "ten" below the line in the tens column.

7 tens + 4 tens + 1 ten = 12 tens.

Put the 2 tens in the answer.

Record the "hundred" below the line in the hundreds column.

Add the hundreds.

4 Do these, using the shorter way of recording.

a 485
  +276

b 392
  +288

c 640
  +272

d 723
  +190

e 635
  + 84

f 186
  +235

1 Try these addition problems.

Be sure to put the figures in the correct columns. The first one is set out for you.

a Add four hundred and four,   404
          forty-four,   44
          fourteen.   + 14
                      ——

b Add five hundred and fifty, fifteen, fifty-five.
c Find the total of forty-six, fifty-six, sixty-six.
d Add one hundred and eight, eighty, eighteen.

Write the answers to these.

2 a I more than 199   **b** 20 less than 112   **c** 2 more than 85
   d Find the total of your answers to **a**, **b**, and **c**.

3 a 2 less than 201   **b** 20 less than 102   **c** 200 less than 320
   d Find the total of your answers to **a**, **b** and **c**.

4 a At Woodlands Infant School there are 84 girls and 103 boys.
   How many children are there at the Infant School?
   b At Woodlands Junior School there are 159 girls and 142 boys.
   How many children are there in the Junior School?
   c How many boys are there altogether in the Infant and Junior School?
   d How many girls are there altogether in the Infant and Junior School?
   e What is the total number of children in both schools?

5 Find out about the number of children in your school and answer
questions like those in **4**.

6 Work out the missing numbers in these magic squares:

a

136	17	
	85	119
68	153	

b

181	27	38	148
	126	115	
104		71	137
49	159	170	16

Chapter 6: Co-ordinates

Routes

This diagram shows a route marked from **A** to **B** moving along the lines. The side of a square is 1 unit.

1 a How long is this route?
   b Is this the **shortest** route along the lines?
   c Is there more than one shortest route?

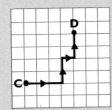

2 a How long is this route?
   b On a small piece of squared paper draw a route 7 units long.
   c Draw a route 9 units long.

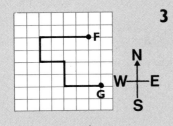

3 This diagram shows one way of getting from **G** to **F** travelling along the lines.
   a How long is it?
   b How long is the shortest route?
   Using the points of the compass we can write this route as 3 West, 2 North, 2 West, 2 North, 4 East or 3W, 2N, 2W, 2N, 4E.

c Find three other ways of getting from **G** to **F**.
  Write down in your book the directions your routes took.
d Write down a route from **F** to **G** in which all the letters N,E,W,S are used.

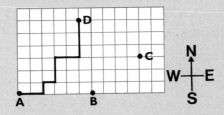

4 The route from **A** to **D** can be written as:
2E, 1N, 1E, 2N, 2E, 3N.

a Copy this route onto squared paper.
b Start at **B** and draw this route on your squared paper: 2N, 1E, 4N, 2W
c Make up a code for yourself showing any route you could use to get from **C** to **B**. (It does not matter if it touches another route.)

Finding a point

Street guides only say what square a street is in.
If we number lines instead of spaces, then our addresses
will be points where the lines cross.

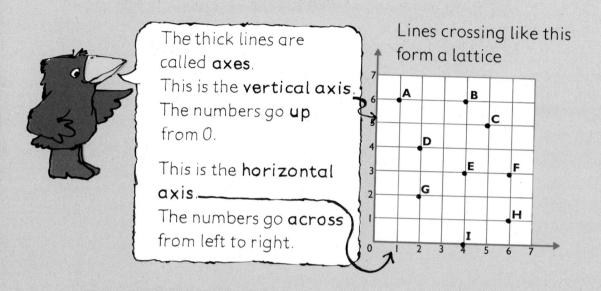

The thick lines are called **axes**.
This is the **vertical axis**.
The numbers go **up** from 0.

This is the **horizontal axis**.
The numbers go **across** from left to right.

Lines crossing like this form a lattice

I These addresses at exact points are called **co-ordinates**.
Start at 0, the **origin**. Count the lines across and then up.
Here the co-ordinates of **A** are (1,6) or 1 across, 6 up,
B is at (4,6), **C** is at (5,5).
Write in your book the co-ordinates of **D**, **E**, **F**, **G**, **H** and **I**.

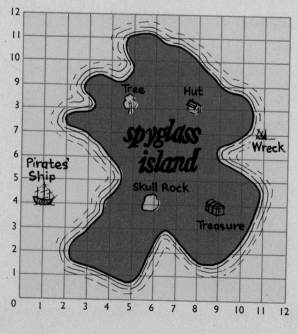

Here is a map of Spyglass Island.
The pirates used it to find
the buried treasure.

2   Write in your book the
co-ordinates of:

a the pirates' ship
b Skull Rock
c the tree
d the hut
e the wreck
f the treasure.

Here is another map.
Look at it and see if you can answer these questions about it.

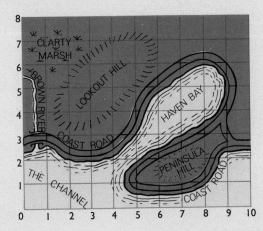

I a Would a good place for a
lighthouse be at (7,2)?

b If my car was at (5,3), would
I be annoyed?

c To go from (3,2) to (5,1) would it
be shorter to go by car or boat?

d Could someone at (2,7) see
someone at (7,3)?

2 Make up your own map, and write a story to go with it.

Joining points

Make a lattice like this on squared paper. Number the lines, not the spaces.
Number the horizontal axis (left to right) from
0 to 12 and the vertical axis (bottom to top) from 0 to 8.

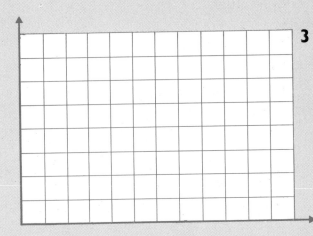

3 Mark these points on your
lattice and join each to the point
which follows it. Inside each
shape, write its name.

a (7,6) (12,6) (8,8) (7,6)

b (10,0) (12,3) (9,5) (7,2) (10,0)

c (4,7) (6,1) (1,5) (7,5) (2,1) (4,7)

4 Make another lattice on squared paper like the last one.
Mark and join these points in order:
(4,7) (2,7) (1,6) (0,4) (2,3) (3,4) (4,3) (4,0) (5,0) (5,2) (6,3) (9,3) (10,2)
(10,0) (11,0) (11,2) (12,4) (12,5) (9,8) (8,7) (9,7) (10,6) (5,6) (4,7) (3,5) (2,7)
Make up another picture and give to your friends the list of co-ordinates
from which to draw the picture.

Chapter 7: Money 1

The pound

1 Look at this pound note.
Whose picture do you see on
the front of it?
Whose picture is on the back?

2 If you look closely at a pound note, using a magnifying glass,
you can see how difficult it would be to copy.
Why is it made difficult to copy?

The £1 coin was introduced on 21st April 1983.
It has exactly the same value as a £1 note.

3 What is written round the edge of the £1 coin?

What does it mean?

How £1 is made up

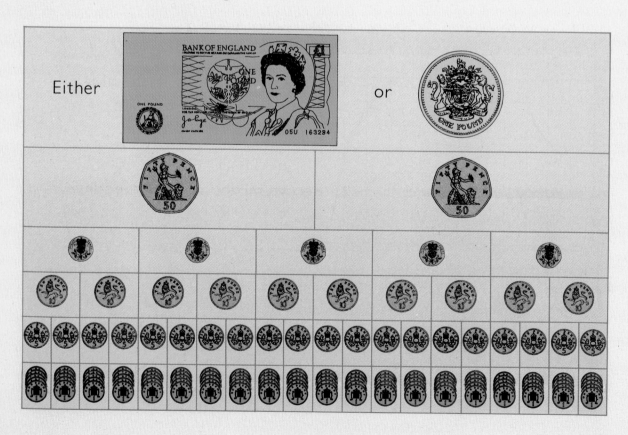

l Copy and complete these sentences.

    a ☐ 50p coins have the same value as £1.

    b ☐ 10p coins have the same value as £1.

    c ☐ 5p coins have the same value as £1.

    d ☐ 10p coins have the same value as a 50p coin.

    e ☐ 5p coins have the same value as a 50p coin.

    f 10 1p coins have the same value as ☐ 5p coins.

    g 30 1p coins have the same value as ☐ 10p coins.

Reading amounts more than £l

To buy things, you often need a mixture of pounds and pence.
When recording, the pounds and pence are kept separate.

Here we have
one pound
and 34 pence.

This is recorded as £1·34.

The decimal point separates the pounds from the pence
and we do not write p after the pence.

Here is another example:

Three pounds and 67 pence
is written as £3·67.

2 Record the following in the same way.

    a One pound and 23 pence.

    b Three pounds and 18 pence.

    c Two pounds and 52 pence.

    d Five pounds and 81 pence.

    e Three pounds and 80 pence.

    f Seven pounds and 14 pence.

    g Four pounds and 58 pence.

    h Ten pounds and 79 pence.

Recording money on an abacus

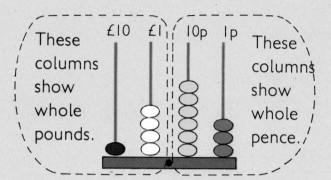

These columns show whole pounds.

These columns show whole pence.

The abacus shows
one £10 and four £1s,
six 10 pences and three pence.
That makes fourteen pounds
and sixty-three pence.

We record it as £14·63

1   Write down the amounts shown on each abacus.

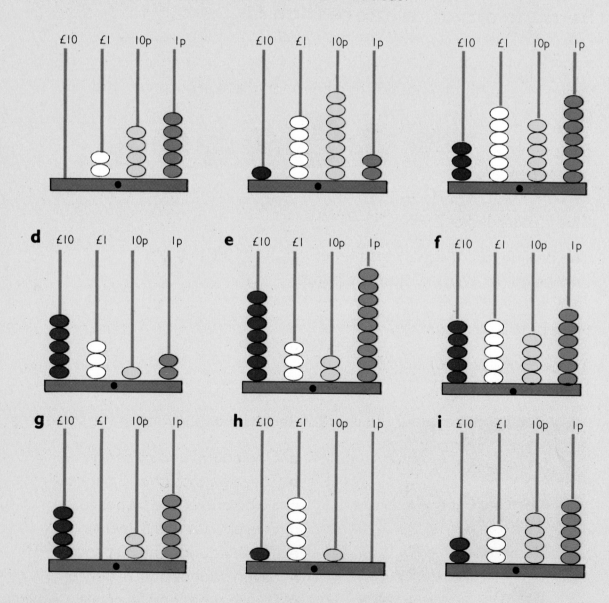

2   Draw an abacus to record each of the following prices.
   a £2·34   **b** £4·23   **c** £16·81   **d** £6·38   **e** £14·64

Giving change up to £1

If you spend 38p in a shop and give the shopkeeper £1 in payment,
he must give you some change.
He usually does it this way.

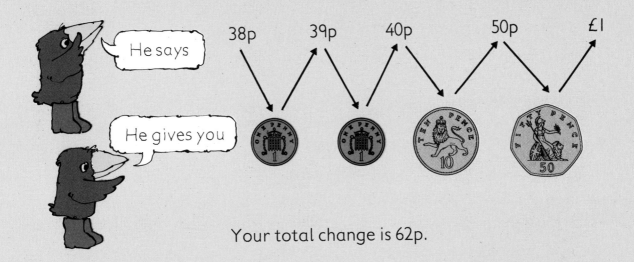

He says   38p   39p   40p   50p   £1

He gives you

Your total change is 62p.

1 What change do you get from £1 if you spend
the following amounts?
Use your coins. The first one is done for you.

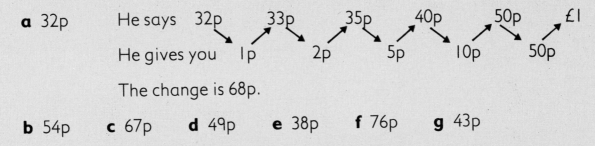

a 32p   He says   32p   33p   35p   40p   50p   £1

He gives you   1p   2p   5p   10p   50p

The change is 68p.

b 54p   **c** 67p   **d** 49p   **e** 38p   **f** 76p   **g** 43p

2 Copy and complete the following additions.

a £1·23
  +£2·34

b £3·81
  +£2·45

c £1·53
  +£3·42

d £2·79
  +£3·50

e £4·53
  +£2·45

f £4·32
  +£1·89

g £3·72
  +£2·19

h £6·23
  +£3·49

i £13·27
  +£ 9·46

j £16·73
  +£19·48

k £13·91
  +£ 8·49

l £17·44
  +£34·78

Chapter 8: Volume and Capacity 1

How much is 100ml?

Here is a big measuring jug, full of fruit drink, and some small glasses. The jug holds 1 litre. Each glass holds 100 millilitres (100ml).

When a glass is filled from the jug, the level in the jug goes down like this:

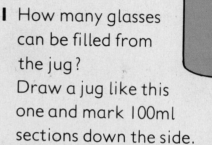

1 How many glasses can be filled from the jug?
   Draw a jug like this one and mark 100ml sections down the side.

Using the 100ml measure

Take a 100ml measure and five milk bottles.
Use the measure and a funnel to put water in the bottles:

100ml in bottle 1
200ml in bottle 2
300ml in bottle 3
400ml in bottle 4
500ml in bottle 5

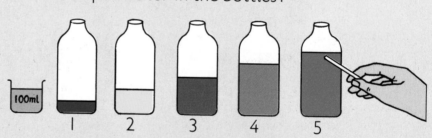

(If you tap them with a pencil you can play a tune.)

2 In your book, write down the total amounts in:
   a bottles 1 and 3
   b bottles 3 and 5
   c bottles 1, 3 and 4
   d bottles 2, 3 and 5

3 a How much more is in bottle 5 than in bottle 3?
   b How much more is in bottle 4 than in bottle 2?
   c How much must you pour from bottle 3 into bottle 1, so that there will be the same amount in bottles 1, 2 and 3?

Very small measures

A hollow cube with sides 1 centimetre long
holds 1 millilitre.

That is why this very small amount is sometimes
called 1 cubic centimetre.

This should be written as 1cm³.

Capacities are sometimes measured in cubic centimetres,
for example the size of motor bike or car engines.

The amount of space something takes up is called its **volume**.
The volume of this cube is 1cm³.

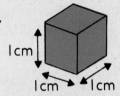

1cm
1cm   1cm

1 Use centimetre cubes to build these solids.
Find their volumes in cm³ by counting the cubes:

a   **b** 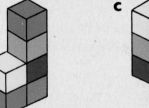   **c** 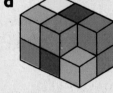   **d**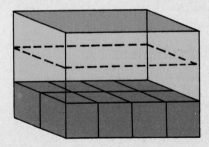

There are 8 cm³ in the bottom layer.
There is room for 3 layers.
8 × 3 = 24
so the box holds 24 cm³.

2 Use centimetre cubes to find how many cm³ these boxes will hold.

a 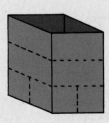   **b** 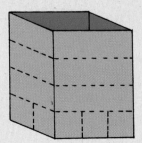   **c**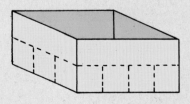

1 A medicine spoon holds 5ml.

Estimate first then use a medicine spoon to measure the capacity of small containers in millilitres.

Record like this:

container	estimate	measure
egg cup wine glass yoghurt pot	ml	ml

2 How many ml of medicine would you swallow, if you took:

a 1 spoonful a day for 5 days? **c** 2 spoonfuls a day for a week?

b 2 spoonfuls a day for 5 days? **d** 3 spoonfuls a day for 10 days?

3 Copy and complete

a 20ml of medicine is ☐ 5ml spoonfuls.

b 15ml of medicine is ☐ 5ml spoonfuls.

c 50ml of medicine is ☐ 5ml spoonfuls.

d 100ml of medicine is ☐ 5ml spoonfuls.

Look at the labels of some medicine bottles and find out how many spoonfuls they hold.

4 Copy and complete

size of bottle	50ml	100ml	150ml	200ml	300ml	500ml
number of 5ml spoonfuls						

The hollow centimetre cube (1ml) and the medicine spoon (5ml) are too small for measuring the capacity of most containers.

You would have to use the hollow cm cube about 270 times or the spoon about 54 times to fill a beaker!

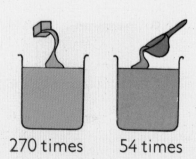

270 times   54 times

Making a 100ml measure

A handy size for a measure is
100 millilitres (100ml) or 100 cubic centimetres (100cm³).

Use 1cm cubes or Cuisenaire rods
to see what 100cm³ looks like.

First make a square layer 5cm by 5cm.

Four layers like this make 100cm³ or 100ml.   4 layers: $25 \times 4 = 100$cm³

To make 100ml measure, cut the top from
an empty plastic container (washing-up liquid bottle).

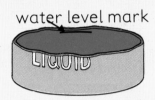

water level mark

LIQUID

Pour 100ml of water from a measuring jug into the
container.

Carefully mark the water level, empty the water out
and cut round the container on the mark.

plastic container
cut to hold 100ml.

You can make a 100ml measure from
card or centimetre squared paper:

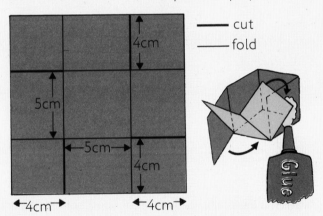

4cm

5cm

5cm

4cm

4cm   4cm

— cut
— fold

Glue

I When you have made your
measure, use it with some
sand to find the capacity of:

a a jam jar   **b** a beaker
c a small box

Record the results in
your book.

1 litre (1000ml) of water weighs 1kg (1000 grams).

1ml of water weighs 1 gram.

100ml of water weighs 1 hecto (100 grams).

If your 100ml container holds water,
weigh it and see.
(It may not quite balance because of the weight
of the container.)

Chapter 9: Place Value 2

Grouping in fives: subtraction

One day Mr Sweet wanted 4 choc-bars for prizes at a party.
In the store he had 2 boxes of 5 choc-bars and 1 single choc-bar.

I want to take away 4 bars, so I must open up a box.
Now I have 1 box and 6 bars.

I can take away 4 bars.
That leaves 1 box and 2 bars.

	boxes	bars
	2	1
	1	6
	—	4
	1	2

1 Set out 5-rods (or base 5 longs) for boxes and units for choc-bars to do these "take away" problems for Mr Sweet.
The first one is done for you with a picture.

	boxes	bars
	2	3
	1	8
	—	4
	1	4

a

boxes	bars
2	3
−	4
1	4

b

boxes	bars
3	1
−	2

c

boxes	bars
4	2
− 1	3

d

boxes	bars
2	0
−	4

e

boxes	bars
3	3
− 2	4

Grouping in sixes: subtraction

Mrs Giles wanted 5 eggs to make a cake. She had 2 boxes and 3 eggs.

> I want to take away 5 eggs so I must open up a box. Now I have 1 box and 9 eggs.
> I can take away 5 eggs.
> That leaves 1 box and 4 eggs.

		boxes	eggs
	o o o	2	3
	o o o o o o o o o	1	9
	o o o o	—	5
	o o o o	1	4

I Set out 6-rods for boxes (or base 6 longs) and units for eggs to do these "take away" problems for Mrs Giles.

a boxes eggs	**b** boxes eggs	**c** boxes eggs	**d** boxes eggs
2 4	3 2	4 1	3 0
− 5	− 4	− 2 3	− 1 5

Using the multi-base board for subtraction

John is using squares, longs and units on the base 4 set.

A long is made from 4 units.

A square is made from 4 longs.

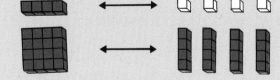

He sets these out on the multi-base board.

He takes away 1 long and 2 units.

This is the answer.

squares	longs	units		He records:
				S L U
				1 3 3
				− 1 2
				1 2 1

How could John do this one?

```
  S  L  U
  1  2  1
-       3
  _____
  _____
```

Set out the pieces and see if you can do it.
(Remember how Mr Sweet and Mrs Giles
did their 'take away' problems.)

He records:

squares	longs	units

John wants to take
away 3 units.

```
  S  L  U

  1  2  1
```

There are not enough
units, so he changes
1 long for 4 units.

```
  1  1  5
```

Now he can take away
3 units.

```
-       3
```

This is the answer.

```
  1  1  2
```

I Use a multi-base board with squares, longs and units (base 4) to do these:

a
```
  S  L  U
  2  2  3
-    1  1
  _____
```

c
```
  S  L  U
  1  1  2
-       3
  _____
```

e
```
  S  L  U
  3  3  1
-    2  2
  _____
```

g
```
  S  L  U
  2  2  3
-    3  1
  _____
```

b
```
  S  L  U
  1  3  2
-    1  3
  _____
```

d
```
  S  L  U
  2  3  2
-    2  3
  _____
```

f
```
  S  L  U
  2  2  2
-    3  3
  _____
```

h
```
  S  L  U
  2  0  0
-    1  2
  _____
```

In base five

A long is made from 5 units.

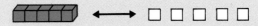

A square is made from 5 longs.

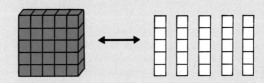

1 Use a multi-base board, squares, long and units (base 5) for these:

a S	L	U
1	4	1
–		3

b S	L	U
2	3	3
–		4

c S	L	U
2	4	2
–	2	4

d S	L	U
2	2	4
–	3	1

In base ten

A long is made from 10 units.

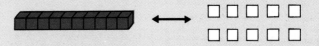

A square is made from 10 longs.

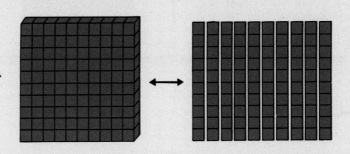

2 Use a multi-base board and squares, long and units in the base 10 set.

a S	L	U
	7	4
–	3	2

c S	L	U
	3	4
–	1	8

e S	L	U
	6	0
–	2	4

g S	L	U
2	3	2
–	4	7

b S	L	U
3	2	7
–	4	3

d S	L	U
1	1	1
–	5	5

f S	L	U
4	2	4
–2	6	5

h S	L	U
4	0	0
–2	3	6

Subtraction on the abacus

For example: 17—4.

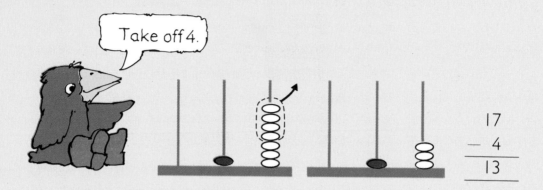

$$\begin{array}{r} 17 \\ -\ 4 \\ \hline 13 \end{array}$$

This is how 23—6 is done on the abacus.

Start with 23.   Not enough units to take off 6, so exchange a "ten" bead for ten units.   Take away 6.   Put the other 4 with the 3 units. This leaves 17.

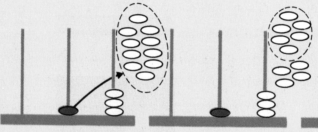

$$\begin{array}{r} 23 \\ -\ 6 \\ \hline 17 \end{array}$$

I Use your abacus to do these subtractions.
   Draw an abacus picture in your answer when you write it in your book.

a 19—6	**e** 44—1 ten	**i** thirty-one—2	**m** 61—eleven
b 27—5	**f** 35—twenty	**j** fifty-six—16	**n** 70—5 tens
c 20—1	**g** 46—33	**k** 19—eleven	**o** 11—1
d 24—6	**h** 48—twenty-four	**l** 90—eleven	**p** 76—67

2 Take 10 from each of these numbers:

   a 17   **b** 19   **c** 30   **d** 51   **e** 36   **f** ninety   **g** 88   **h** 10

Chapter 10: Subtraction 1

Subtracting tens and units

1 Do these subtraction problems in your book.

a 46	**b** 37	**c** 88	**d** 65	**e** 99
−25	−13	−34	−44	−73

Splitting tens

Sometimes there are not enough units in the top number,
so a ten has to be exchanged for 10 units.

Mary has 32p and John has no money. Mary wants to give 17p to John.

There are not enough ⬤ coins.	She changes 1 ⬤ coin for 10 ⬤ coins.	She gives 17p to John.	She has 15p left.

 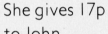 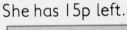

 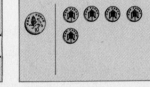

$$(30+2) \longrightarrow (20+12) \longrightarrow \begin{array}{r} (20+12) \\ -(10+\ 7) \\ \hline (10+\ 5) \end{array} \longrightarrow 15p$$

Using ten-rods and units, the problem looks like this:

Start with 32.	There are not enough units, so exchange 1 rod for 10 units.	Take away 17.	15 are left.

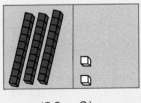 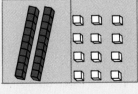 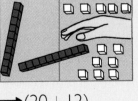 

$$(30+2) \longrightarrow (20+12) \longrightarrow \begin{array}{r} (20+12) \\ -(10+\ 7) \\ \hline (10+\ 5) \end{array} \longrightarrow 15$$

Use ten-rods and units like this for 53 — 26.

Start with 53.

There are not enough units, so exchange 1 rod for 10 units.

Take away 26.

27 are left.

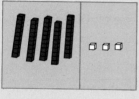 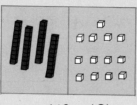  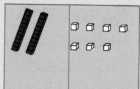

$(50+3)$ $(40+13)$

$(40+13)$
$-(20+6)$
$\overline{(20+7)}$ $=$ 27

1   Now try these. Set them out in the same way.

a 36	b 75	c 64	d 50	e 44	f 52
−19	−48	−29	−17	−35	−9

Here is a shorter way of setting out:

```
53
−29
───
```

There are not enough units so exchange a 10.
$50+3$ becomes $40+13$.

```
4  13
$  $
−2  9
─────
2  4
```

2   These have been started for you. Copy and complete.

```
   4 13      2 16      8 12      5 16      4 10      7 13
a  $ $    b $ $    c $ $    d $ $    e $ $    f $ $
  −1 7     −1 9     −6 5     −3 9     −2 2     −1 9
```

3   Try these. Set them out in the same way.

a 53	c 86	e 55	g 80	i 73	k 73
−18	−37	−26	−36	−47	−65

b 72	d 67	f 70	h 73	j 73	l 47
−49	−48	−52	−38	−56	−28

Subtracting hundreds, tens and units

Start with 256.   Take away 124.

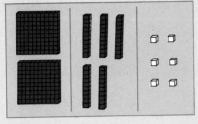 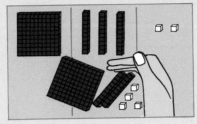 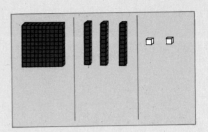

$$200 + 50 + 6 \longrightarrow \begin{array}{r} (200+50+6) \\ -(100+20+4) \\ \hline 100+30+2 \end{array} = \quad 132$$

I Copy and complete:

a $\begin{array}{r} 275 \\ -143 \end{array}$ $\begin{array}{r} (200+ \quad + \quad) \\ -(100+ 40 + 3) \\ \hline 100+ \quad + \quad = \end{array}$

b $\begin{array}{r} 366 \\ - 52 \end{array}$ $\begin{array}{r} (300+ \quad + \quad) \\ -(\quad 50 + 2) \\ \hline + \quad + \quad = \end{array}$

2 Set these out the same way:

a $\begin{array}{r} 456 \\ -234 \end{array}$
b $\begin{array}{r} 477 \\ - 73 \end{array}$
c $\begin{array}{r} 327 \\ -117 \end{array}$
d $\begin{array}{r} 188 \\ - 60 \end{array}$
e $\begin{array}{r} 453 \\ -320 \end{array}$
f $\begin{array}{r} 580 \\ -310 \end{array}$

Splitting tens again

$265 - 137$

Start with 265.

There are not enough units so exchange a ten for 10 units.

Take away 137.

$$200 + 60 + 5 \longrightarrow 200 + 50 + 15 \longrightarrow \begin{array}{r} (200+50+15) \\ -(100+30+ 7) \\ \hline 100+20+ 8 \end{array} = 128$$

1 Use squares, ten-rods and units.
Copy and complete.

a   273 ⟶ (200+70+3) ⟶ (200+ 60 +   )
        −146 ⟶ (100+40+6) ⟶ (100+ 40 + 6)
        ⟵─────────────── (100+   +   )

b   281 ⟶ (200+80+1) ⟶ (200+   +   )
        − 67 ⟶ −(60+7) ⟶ −(60 + 7)
        ⟵─────────────── (200+   +   )

2 Set these out in the same way.

a 341   **b** 176   **c** 322   **d** 460   **e** 385   **f** 743
     −138   − 49   −108   − 36   −179   −534

Now try the shorter way:

   273   ⁶ ¹³
  −158   Not enough units   2 7̸ 3̸
  ─────   so exchange a ten.   −1 5 8
                                                 ──────
                                                 1 1 5

3 These have been started for you. Copy and complete.

   ⁴ ¹⁴   ⁶ ¹²   ⁵ ¹⁰   ² ¹⁵   ¹ ¹⁷   ² ¹³
a 2 8̸ 4̸ **b** 5 7̸ 2̸ **c** 8 6̸ 0̸ **d** 4 3̸ 5̸ **e** 3 2̸ 7̸ **f** 5 3̸ 3̸
   −1 2 9   −3 4 6   −3 2 4   −1 0 8   −1 1 9   5 1 7
   ──────   ──────   ──────   ──────   ──────   ──────

4 Set these out the shortest way:

a 342   **c** 760   **e** 873   **g** 217   **i** 550   **k** 241
     −125   −232   − 59   −108   − 27   −109
     ────   ────   ────   ────   ────   ────

b 492   **d** 342   **f** 470   **h** 635   **j** 740   **l** 753
     − 47   −136   −436   −219   −332   −246
     ────   ────   ────   ────   ────   ────

Chapter 11: Weight 1

Using smaller weights

You often need to use several different sizes of
weight together to balance something.

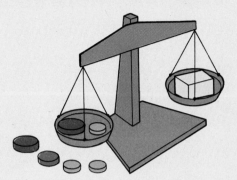

1 What do these weights add up to? Copy and complete.

    a 10g + 10g + 10g = ☐ g   **d** 20g + 20g + 20g + 10g = ☐ g

    b 20g + 10g + 10g = ☐ g   **e** 50g + 10g + 10g + 10g = ☐ g

    c 20g + 20g + 20g = ☐ g   **f** 50g + 20g + 10g = ☐ g

2 Copy and complete this table showing how to make different totals using 50g, 20g and 10g weights.

	50g	20g	10g	total
a	1	1	1	80 g
b	0	1	1	☐ g
c	1	1	0	☐ g
d	0	1	2	☐ g

	50g	20g	10g	total
e	1	0	1	☐ g
f	1	2	1	☐ g
g	1	0	2	☐ g
h	0	3	2	☐ g

3 Now weigh some real things using different sized weights as you need them.
Estimate the weight first and record like this:

object	estimate	weight
book	☐ g	☐ g
cup	☐ g	☐ g

4 There are lots of ways of making smaller weights add up to 100g.
Copy and complete:

    a 60g + ☐ g = 100g   **c** 30g + ☐ g = 100g

    b ☐ g + 50g = 100g   **d** 20g + 20g + ☐ g = 100g

5 Now try subtracting weights. Copy and complete.

    a 100g − 40g = ☐ g   **c** 100g − 30g = ☐ g

    b 100g − ☐ g = 20g   **d** ☐ g − 50g = 50g

Weighing more accurately

Using 100g weights,
we find a book weighs
more than 100g
but less than 200g.

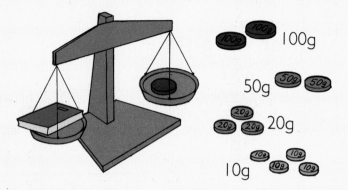

Start with a 100g weight then add a 50g weight.
If the book still does not balance add smaller
weights till the book balances. Keep counting the
total weight as you go; this is called 'counting on'.

Steps

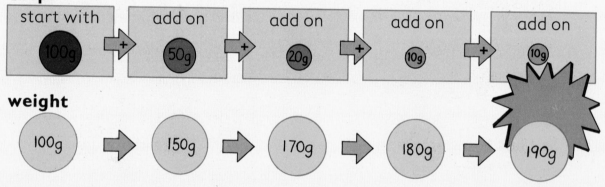

total correct
weight of book.

1 Practise counting on with these examples.
Write down the total weight after each step.
The first one is done for you in full, complete the others in the same way.

a Steps   100g + 50g + 10g + 10g
Weight   100g → 150g → 160g → 170g total

b 100g + 50g + 20g + 10g

c 100g + 20g + 20g + 10g + 10g

d 100g + 50g + 10g + 10g + 10g

e 100g + 20g + 10g + 10g

f 100g + 100g + 20g + 20g

g 100g + 100g + 100g + 50g + 10g

h 100g + 100g + 50g + 20g

i 100g + 100g + 20g + 10g

Suppose you have a panful of jumbled weights to count.
Pick out the heaviest first then the next heaviest
and count on till you reach the total.

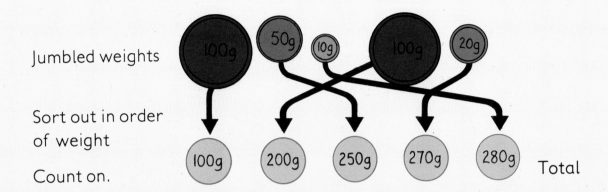

Jumbled weights

Sort out in order
of weight

Count on.

Total

1 Copy these jumbles into your book and
sort them out in the same way.

a

b

c

d

e This one is recorded as
1 kg and ☐ g.

Weighing in kilograms and grams

2 Use the scales to weigh some things that you think weigh about 1 kg.
Estimate the weight first.
Record the estimates and correct weights in a table like this:

object	estimate kg	g	weight kg	g
dictionary	1	200	0	970
bottle	0	750	1	40
and so on. . . .				

Chapter 12: Subtraction 2

Splitting hundreds

This time, token cards are used to show: 324 − 152

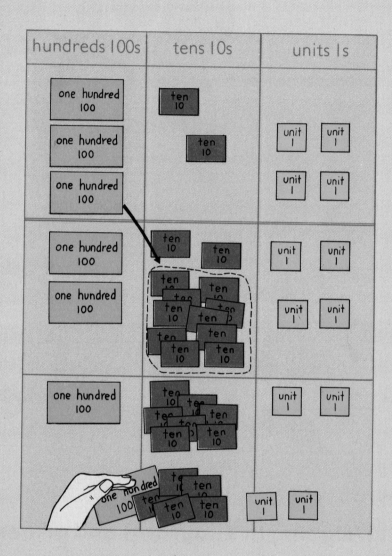

Start with 324:
   3 100 s + 2 10 s + 4 1 s

To take away 152:
   1 100 + 5 10 s + 2 1 s
there are enough 1 s
but not enough 10 s.

Exchange a 100 token
for ten 10 s.
   3 100 s + 2 10 s + 4 1 s

   2 100 s + 12 10 s + 4 1 s

Take away
(1 100 + 5 10 + 2 1)

Record like this: 324 ⟶ (200 + 120 + 4)
                   − 152 ⟶ − (100 + 50 + 2)
                    172 ⟵   (100 + 70 + 2)

I   Use squares, longs and units or token cards for these.
Set them out in the same way.

a 346 − 180   **c** 408 − 276   **e** 525 − 281   **g** 308 − 124
b 210 − 90   **d** 520 − 218   **f** 216 − 170   **h** 672 − 492

The shorter way of setting out can be used:

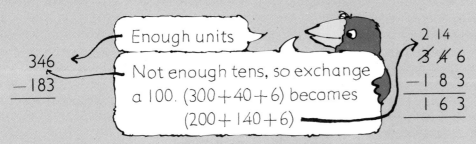

$$\begin{array}{r} 346 \\ -183 \\ \hline \end{array}$$

Enough units

Not enough tens, so exchange a 100. (300+40+6) becomes (200+140+6)

$$\begin{array}{r} {}^{2\ 14} \\ \cancel{3}\ \cancel{4}\ 6 \\ -1\ 8\ 3 \\ \hline 1\ 6\ 3 \\ \end{array}$$

1 These have been started for you. Copy and complete.

a
```
  1 12
  2 2 0
 −   8 0
```
c
```
  7 10
  8 0 0
 −3 9 0
```
e
```
  8 11
  9 1 8
 −2 7 0
```
g
```
  2 10
  8 0 7
 −1 7 6
```
i
```
  6 10
  7 0 8
 −5 8 8
```

b
```
  3 13
  4 3 0
 −1 7 0
```
d
```
  3 12
  4 2 4
 −2 8 3
```
f
```
  6 18
  7 8 2
 −  9 0
```
h
```
  3 12
  4 2 6
 −1 5 6
```
j
```
  7 17
  8 1 5
 −3 8 2
```

2 Try these. Set them out in the same way:

a
```
 430
− 60
```
c
```
 876
−492
```
e
```
 752
−280
```
g
```
 363
−281
```
i
```
 308
−238
```
k
```
 429
−218
```

b
```
 281
−190
```
d
```
 500
−330
```
f
```
 907
−645
```
h
```
 405
−265
```
j
```
 666
−484
```
l
```
 728
−688
```

3 Read these carefully. Make sure you know which number to start with and which number to subtract.

a From 283 take 191.

b Take 384 from 509.

c A farmer picks 748kg of apples.
If he sells 560kg how many kg are left?

d By how many is 600 greater than 280?

e 882 is less than 909 by how many?

f Subtract 186 from 306.

g John had 205 stamps but gave away 92. How many were left?

h Anne needs 315 points to win a game. She scores 175.
How many more points does she need?

Splitting hundreds and tens

Look at these pictures
for 223 — 45.

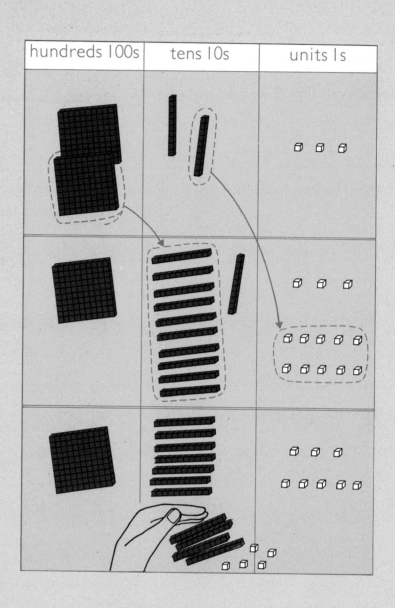

hundreds 100s	tens 10s	units 1s

Start with 223.
2 (100) + 2 (10) + 3 (1)

To take away 45:
4 (10) + 5 (1)
there are not enough 1's
and not enough 10s.

Exchange a 10 rod for
10 units and a 100 square
for ten 10-rods.

Now you can
take away 45.

Record like this:

$$223 \longrightarrow (200 + 10 + 13) \longrightarrow (100 + 110 + 13)$$
$$- 45 \longrightarrow - (40 + 5) \longrightarrow - (40 + 5)$$
$$178 \longleftarrow (100 + 70 + 8)$$

I Use squares, longs and units or token cards for these:

a 334 — 57	**c** 355 — 168	**e** 846 — 288	**g** 645 — 456
b 245 — 79	**d** 260 — 186	**f** 552 — 85	**h** 200 — 38

The last question **h** is a little different because when you tried
to exchange a ten there weren't any tens. What did you do?

For 200 — 38:

Start with 200.
There are not enough units
or tens to take away 38.
First exchange a 100 for
ten 10-rods.

Then exchange a ten-rod
for ten units.
Record like this:

hundreds 100s	tens 10s	units 1s

$$
\begin{array}{ll}
200 & (100+90+10) \\
-\ 38 & -\quad\ (30+\ 8) \\
\hline
162 & (100+60+\ 2)
\end{array}
$$

Here is the shorter way of setting out when hundreds
and tens have to be split.

234 Not enough units. Exchange a 10.
− 58

$$
\begin{array}{r}
{}^{2\ \ 14} \\
2\ \cancel{3}\ \cancel{4} \\
-\ 5\ 8 \\
\hline
6
\end{array}
$$

Not enough tens. Exchange a 100.

$$
\begin{array}{r}
{}^{1\ \ 12\ \ 14} \\
\cancel{2}\ \cancel{3}\ \cancel{4} \\
-\quad 5\ 8 \\
\hline
1\ 7\ 6
\end{array}
$$

1 These have been started for you. Copy and complete.

$$
\mathbf{a}\ \begin{array}{r} {}^{2\ 11\ 16} \\ \cancel{3}\cancel{2}\cancel{6} \\ -\ \ 4\ 8 \\ \hline \end{array}
\quad
\mathbf{b}\ \begin{array}{r} {}^{3\ 13\ 14} \\ \cancel{4}\cancel{4}\cancel{4} \\ -1\ 5\ 6 \\ \hline \end{array}
\quad
\mathbf{c}\ \begin{array}{r} {}^{4\ 14\ 15} \\ \cancel{5}\cancel{5}\cancel{5} \\ -2\ 7\ 9 \\ \hline \end{array}
\quad
\mathbf{d}\ \begin{array}{r} {}^{2\ 11\ 14} \\ \cancel{3}\cancel{2}\cancel{4} \\ -1\ 8\ 8 \\ \hline \end{array}
\quad
\mathbf{e}\ \begin{array}{r} {}^{4\ 15\ 13} \\ \cancel{5}\cancel{6}\cancel{3} \\ -\ \ 9\ 5 \\ \hline \end{array}
\quad
\mathbf{f}\ \begin{array}{r} {}^{2\ 9\ 10} \\ \cancel{3}\cancel{0}\cancel{0} \\ -1\ 7\ 6 \\ \hline \end{array}
$$

2 Try these. Set them out the same way.

$$
\mathbf{a}\ \begin{array}{r} 325 \\ -\ 49 \\ \hline \end{array}
\quad
\mathbf{b}\ \begin{array}{r} 666 \\ -278 \\ \hline \end{array}
\quad
\mathbf{c}\ \begin{array}{r} 111 \\ -\ 43 \\ \hline \end{array}
\quad
\mathbf{d}\ \begin{array}{r} 216 \\ -147 \\ \hline \end{array}
\quad
\mathbf{e}\ \begin{array}{r} 742 \\ -\ 55 \\ \hline \end{array}
\quad
\mathbf{f}\ \begin{array}{r} 700 \\ -444 \\ \hline \end{array}
$$

3 Set out each subtraction carefully, then copy and complete
the computer tape.

− 156	500	400	300	200	246	354	462	570	678

4 Write some short number stories which lead to subtraction problems.

Chapter 13: Length 2

Looking at the metre ruler

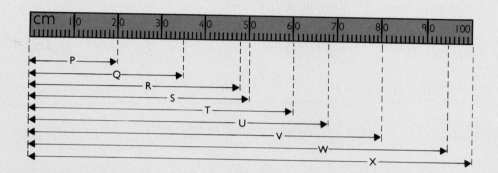

1 Write down the letter for each arrow and its length.
For example: Line P is 20 cm long.

2 Work out the total length of these lines.

    a P and Q   **c** P and V   **e** Q and T   **g** P and T
    b P and S   **d** Q and S   **f** R and T   **h** U and R

The metre, decimetre and centimetre

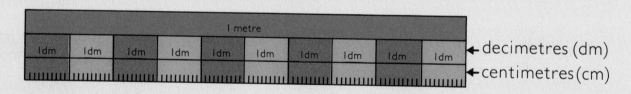

3 Copy and complete:

    a There are ☐ cm in 1 decimetre   **d** There are ☐ cm in 10 decimetres
    b There are ☐ cm in 2 decimetres   **e** There are ☐ decimetres in 1 metre
    c There are ☐ cm in 5 decimetres   **f** There are ☐ cm in one metre

Because there are ten decimetres in one metre,
1 decimetre is a tenth of a metre
$1\,dm = \frac{1}{10}m$

Because there are 100 centimetres in one metre,
1 centimetre is a hundredth of a metre
$1\,cm = \frac{1}{100}m$

Recording measurements on a decimal abacus

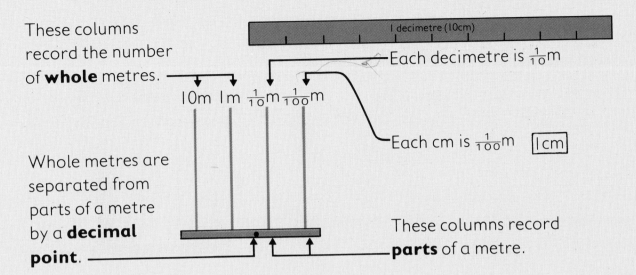

These columns record the number of **whole** metres.

Each decimetre is $\frac{1}{10}$m

Each cm is $\frac{1}{100}$m | 1cm |

10m 1m $\frac{1}{10}$m $\frac{1}{100}$m

Whole metres are separated from parts of a metre by a **decimal point**.

These columns record **parts** of a metre.

This is how 16cm is recorded on the abacus:

$16\text{cm} = 10\text{cm} + 6\text{cm}$

$= \frac{1}{10}\text{m} + \frac{6}{100}\text{m}$

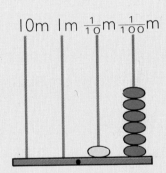

1 Record these in the same way with abacus pictures.

a 14cm	**c** 28cm	**e** 30cm	**g** 99cm
b 23cm	**d** 29cm	**f** 45cm	**h** 100cm

2 Copy and complete.

a 100cm = ☐m	**d** 3m = ☐cm	**g** 1000cm = ☐m	**j** 11m = ☐cm
b 200cm = ☐m	**e** 7m = ☐cm	**h** 1200cm = ☐m	**k** 13m = ☐cm
c 400cm = ☐m	**f** 9m = ☐cm	**i** 3500cm = ☐m	**l** 17m = ☐cm

This is how 214cm can be recorded on an abacus:

$214\,\text{cm} = 200\text{cm} + 10\text{cm} + 4\text{cm}$

$= 2\text{m} + \frac{1}{10}\text{m} + \frac{4}{100}\text{m} = 2.14\text{m}$

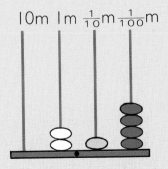

10m 1m $\frac{1}{10}$m $\frac{1}{100}$m

3 Draw an abacus picture for each of these measurements.

    a 316cm   **b** 124cm   **c** 653cm   **d** 302cm   **e** 1440cm **f** 1030cm

I A builder used a metre stick and a decimetre strip to measure lengths of wood.

He recorded the lengths in two ways –

like this:

	m	dm	cm
a	2	1	8
b	6	3	2
c	9	4	6
d	7	5	8
e	1	9	1
f	15	6	0

and like this:

m	cm
2	18

Here is measurement **a** shown on an abacus.

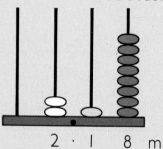

2 · 1   8   m

2m 18cm or 2·18m

Copy and complete the second table and draw abacus pictures for the other measurements.

2 Write the measurements shown by these abacus pictures, first in m and cm then using a decimal point.
For example: **a** 13m 23cm   13·23m

a
10m 1m $\frac{1}{10}$m $\frac{1}{100}$m
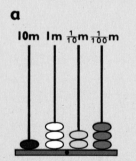

b
10m 1m $\frac{1}{10}$m $\frac{1}{100}$m
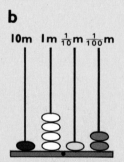

c
10m 1m $\frac{1}{10}$m $\frac{1}{100}$m
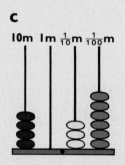

d
10m 1m $\frac{1}{10}$m $\frac{1}{100}$m
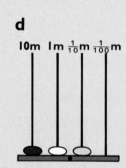

3 Record measurements made in your classroom.
Draw decimal abacus pictures of your results.

object or distance	whole metres	parts of a metre(cm)	metres and parts together
height of a door	1	98	1·98m
width of door			
distance of my desk from door			
height of my friend			

Finding the perimeter

To find the perimeter
of this shape
add the lengths of
the sides together:

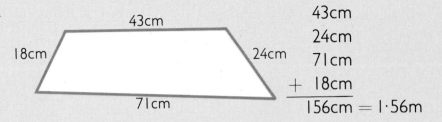

```
  43cm
  24cm
  71cm
+ 18cm
─────────────
 156cm = 1·56m
```

I Find the perimeter of these shapes.

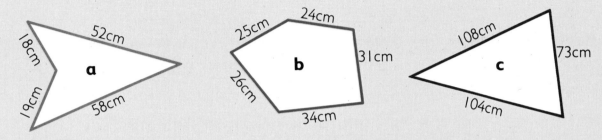

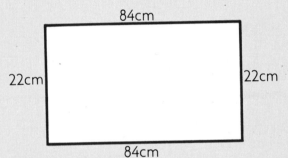

Opposite sides of a rectangle are
the same length, so the perimeter
can be worked out like this:

2 (84cm) + 2 (22cm)

```
  168cm
+  44cm
──────────────
  212cm = 2·12m
```

2 Find the perimeters of these rectangles.

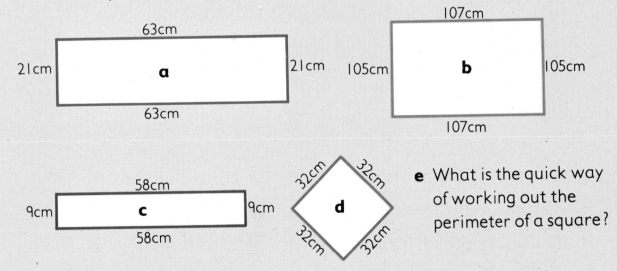

e What is the quick way
of working out the
perimeter of a square?

3 Find the perimeter of six things in your classroom and
record your results.

Using a measuring tape

Always work with a partner.
Lay the tape on the ground and do not let it sag.
Make sure that the tape is running in a straight line.
Roll up the tape immediately after each measurement.
Do not let the tape get wet or muddy.

If we look closely, Section A to B looks like this:

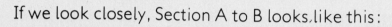

1   Here are some sections taken from a measuring tape.
    Read off and record the measurements shown by the arrows.

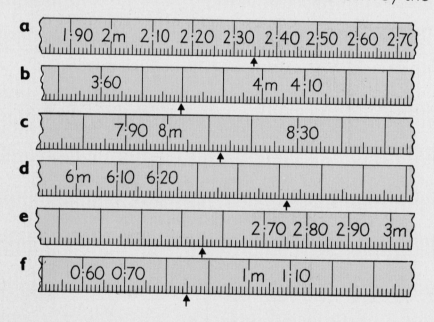

a   1·90 2m 2·10 2·20 2·30 2·40 2·50 2·60 2·70

b   3·60   4m 4·10

c   7·90 8m   8·30

d   6m 6·10 6·20

e   2·70 2·80 2·90 3m

f   0·60 0·70   1m 1·10

2   Use your tape measure to measure and record like this:

	whole metres	decimetre sections	cm over	total m
width of your classroom		·		·
length of a wall		·		·
length of playground		·		·
distance from window to door		·		·

Chapter 14: Multiplication 1

Square numbers up to 100

You have met the first six square numbers.

$1 \times 1 = 1$ $2 \times 2 = 4$ $3 \times 3 = 9$ $4 \times 4 = 16$ $5 \times 5 = 25$ $6 \times 6 = 36$

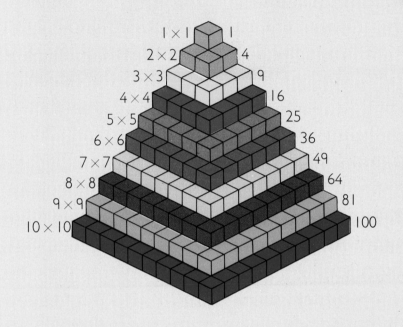

1×1 1
2×2 4
3×3 9
4×4 16
5×5 25
6×6 36
7×7 49
8×8 64
9×9 81
10×10 100

This diagram shows the square numbers up to 100.

Learn these ten square numbers.

1 Square numbers
Differences

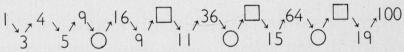

The square numbers make a diagonal on the 10×10 multiplication square.
$5 \times 3 = 3 \times 5$, etc. so
we only need to fill in
one side of the diagonal.
You should know the products in **"Zone A"**,
which is shaded.

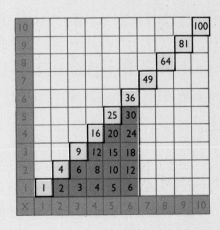

2 Cover the table square then copy and complete.

a $4 \times 4 = \square$ **d** $2 \times 2 = \square$ **g** $4 \times 6 = \square$ **j** $6 \times 3 = \square$ **m** $5 \times \square = 20$

b $5 \times 3 = \square$ **e** $5 \times 5 = \square$ **h** $7 \times 7 = \square$ **k** $9 \times 9 = \square$ **n** $8 \times \square = 64$

c $2 \times 6 = \square$ **f** $4 \times 3 = \square$ **i** $3 \times 6 = \square$ **l** $6 \times 1 = \square$ **o** $6 \times \square = 36$

The next products to be learned are in **Zone B**.

The table of 1's is easy. Any number multiplied by 1 is itself.

Doubling gives the rest of the table of 2's: 14, 16, 18, 20.

The 10's table is easy too: 10, 20, 30, 40, 50, 60, 70, 80, 90

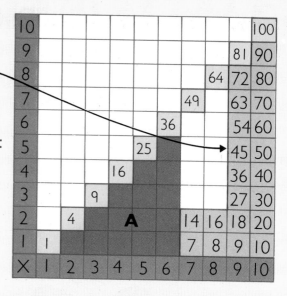

	1	2	3	4	5	6	7	8	9	10
10										100
9									81	90
8								64	72	80
7							49		63	70
6						36			54	60
5					25				45	50
4				16					36	40
3			9						27	30
2		4			**A**			14	16	18	20
1	1						7	8	9	10
X	1	2	3	4	5	6	7	8	9	10

The 9's table has a clear pattern.

$9 \times 1 = 9$	$0 + 9 = 9$
$9 \times 2 = 18$	$1 + 8 = 9$
$9 \times 3 = 27$	$2 + 7 = 9$
$9 \times 4 = 36$	$3 + 6 = 9$
$9 \times 5 = 45$	$4 + 5 = 9$
$9 \times 6 = 54$	$5 + 4 = 9$
$9 \times 7 = 63$	$6 + 3 = 9$
$9 \times 8 = 72$	$7 + 2 = 9$
$9 \times 9 = 81$	$8 + 1 = 9$
$9 \times 10 = 90$	$9 + 0 = 9$

The digits in the product add up to 9.
From each product to the next is "10 up and 1 down". ($+10 - 1$ is the same as $+9$)

The number of tens is 1 less than the number you are multiplying the 9 by.

For example: $9 \times 3 = 2\square$ "Twenty-something"
$\qquad 2 + 7 = 9 \quad$ so $9 \times 3 = 27$

$\qquad\qquad 9 \times 6 = 5\square$ "Fifty-something"
$\qquad\qquad 5 + 4 = 9 \quad$ so $9 \times 6 = 54$

1 Cover Zone B of the table and try these:

a $2 \times 8 = \square$ c $10 \times 7 = \square$ e $9 \times 4 = \square$ g $9 \times \square = 72$ i $10 \times \square = 40$

b $9 \times 1 = \square$ d $9 \times 10 = \square$ f $9 \times 7 = \square$ h $9 \times \square = 81$ j $\square \times 10 = 80$

The 9's table can be shown on your fingers.
For $9 \times \mathbf{4}$, turn down the **4**th finger from the left.
These show the number of tens (3).

These show the numbers of units (6).

$30 + 6 = 36$
$9 \times 4 = 36$

Try it for the rest of the 9's table.

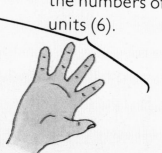

Zone C has only nine products to learn.

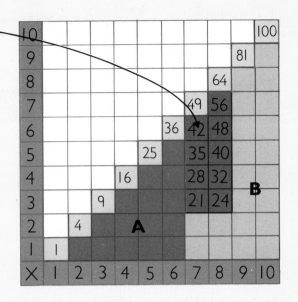

Two of these are part of the easy
5's table.
5, 10, 15, 20, 25, 30, 35, 40, 45, 50.

Two are "double doubles".
$7 \times 4 = 7 \times 2 \times 2 = 14 \times 2 = 28$
$8 \times 4 = 8 \times 2 \times 2 = 32$

The 8's table is "double 4's".
$8 \times 3 = 2(4 \times 3) = 2(12) = 24$
$8 \times 4 = 2(4 \times 4) = 2(16) = 32$
$8 \times 6 = 2(4 \times 6) = 2(24) = 48$
$8 \times 7 = 2(4 \times 7) = 2(28) = 56$

and $7 \times 6 = 2(7 \times 3) = 2(21) = 42$

1 Cover Zone C and try these:
a $7 \times 3 = \square$ **c** $6 \times 8 = \square$ **e** $8 \times 4 = \square$ **g** $5 \times 7 = \square$ **i** $8 \times \square = 56$
b $5 \times 8 = \square$ **d** $7 \times 6 = \square$ **f** $7 \times 8 = \square$ **h** $7 \times 4 = \square$ **j** $7 \times \square = 42$

2 On squared paper, make a multiplication square. Fill the square numbers and Zones A, B, C. Now make a table jig-saw by cutting along the lines. See if your friend can fit it together again.

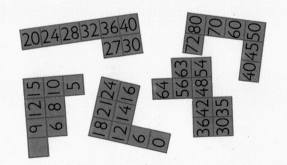

3 Use 100 square number grids to mark table patterns in colour. The picture shows the 7's pattern.

1	2	3	4	5	6	7	8	9	10
11	12	13	14	15	16	17	18	19	20
21	22	23	24	25	26	27	28	29	30
31	32	33	34	35	36	37	38	39	40
41	42	43	44	45	46	47	48	49	50
51	52	53	54	55	56	57	58	59	60

4 When you know your tables, multiplying 20, 30, 40, . . . etc. by units is easy: $30 \times 4 = 3 \times 4 \times 10 = 12 \times 10 = 120$

Try these: **a** $20 \times 4 = \square$ **c** $60 \times 3 = \square$ **e** $80 \times 9 = \square$ **g** $50 \times 6 = \square$
b $30 \times 5 = \square$ **d** $40 \times 7 = \square$ **f** $9 \times 30 = \square$ **h** $8 \times 80 = \square$

Chapter 15: Area

Counting square centimetres

Square units are counted to find the **area** of a surface.
A square with sides of one centimetre has an area of **one square centimetre**.

The area of this rectangle is 6 square centimetres.
To save writing square centimetre in full every time it is
needed, cm² can be written and read as "square centimetre".

1 What is the area, in cm², of these rectangles?

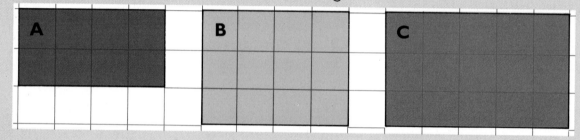

2 It is easy to work out the area of a shape which is half of a rectangle.
Write down the area of these.

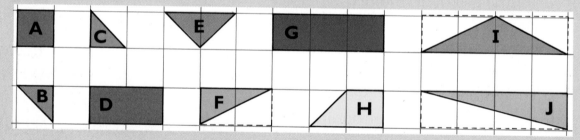

3 Now work out these areas in cm².

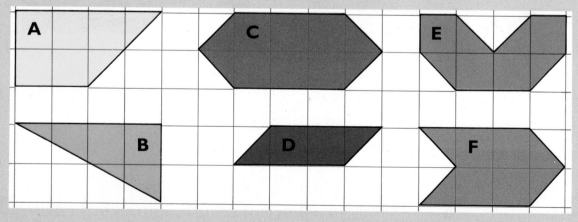

1 Using paper marked in cm², draw shapes which have the following areas:
  a 6 cm²   **b** 10 cm²   **c** 15 cm²   **d** 21 cm²   **e** 19 cm²

2 **a** Draw a rectangle with the same area as the triangle.
  b Draw a square with the same area as the rectangle.

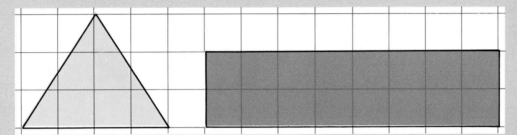

3 On a piece of tracing paper, trace the grid from some one-centimetre squared paper. The traced grid can be used to find the area of a surface by putting it over and counting the squares.

Use the squared tracing paper to find the areas of surfaces such as the front cover of a book or the top of a small box.

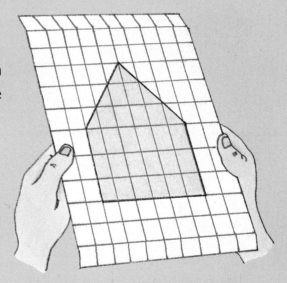

Record in your book like this: The reading book has an area of 300 cm².

Irregular shapes

If we put the tracing paper over a shape like this or copy the shape on to squared paper it does not fit exactly on to grid squares.

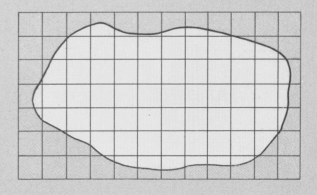

To find its approximate area, count:

24 whole squares (✗)

9 pieces of $\frac{1}{2}$ or more

___ of a square (✓)

33 cm² approximately.

Count as a square if it is more than half.
Do not count if less than half.

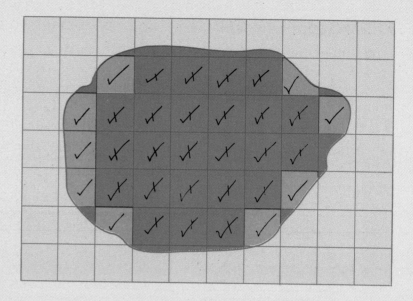

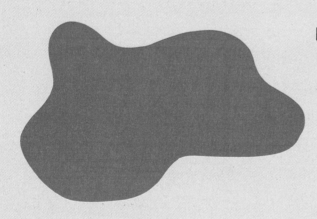

1 **a** Estimate the area, in cm², of this shape.
   b Copy the shape onto a grid of square centimetres.
   c Find its approximate area by counting the squares.
   d How many cm² different was your estimate?

2 Place your hand flat with fingers together on a piece of centimetre squared paper. Draw round your hand and find its approximate area.

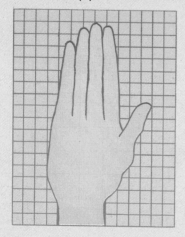

3

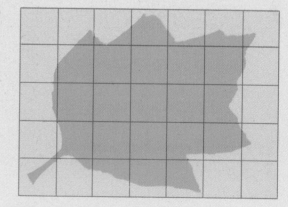

Find the approximate area of this leaf in cm². Make a collection of leaves from different trees. Sort them into order of their areas, starting with the smallest.

Working out areas

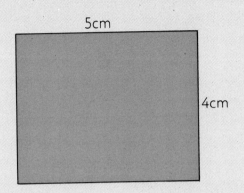

This rectangle is 5cm long and 4cm wide.

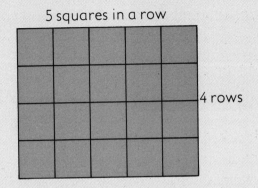

If it is covered with square centimetres there are 5 squares in a row and 4 rows.
The area of the rectangle is 20cm².

If you know the number of squares in a row, and the number of rows, how can you find the number of squares in the area?

l What is the area of each of these rectangles drawn on a centimetre square grid? Record like this: A is 10cm².

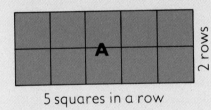

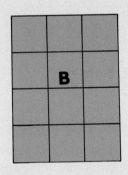

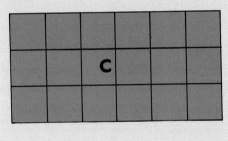

2 Find the areas of these rectangles and record.

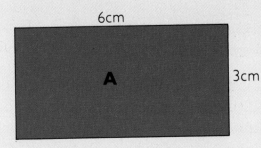

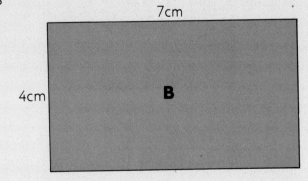

I Measure the sides of these rectangles and then find their areas.

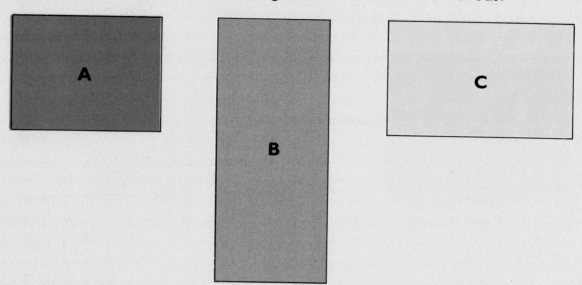

2 Find the areas of these shapes which are made from rectangles.

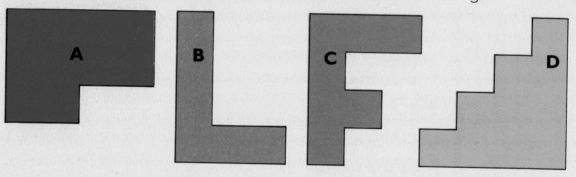

Shapes with the same area

3 You can arrange 24 square centimetres to form different rectangles. Two have been done for you.

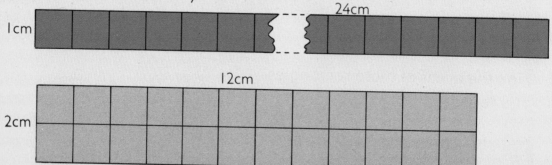

a Make up some more of your own using 24 square centimetres.
b Do the same with 36 square centimetres.
c Do the same with 48 square centimetres.

Chapter 16: Division 1

Checking division on the multiplication square

For $42 \div 7 = \square$, go along the 7 row until you reach 42. 42 is in the 6 column so $42 \div 7 = 6$ because $7 \times 6 = 42$.

10	10	20	30	40	50	60	70	80	90	100
9	9	18	27	36	45	54	63	72	81	90
8	8	16	24	32	40	48	56	64	72	80
7	7	14	21	28	35	42	49	56	63	70
6	6	12	18	24	30	36	42	48	54	60
5	5	10	15	20	25	30	35	40	45	50
4	4	8	12	16	20	24	28	32	36	40
3	3	6	9	12	15	18	21	24	27	30
2	2	4	6	8	10	12	14	16	18	20
1	1	2	3	4	5	6	7	8	9	10
×	1	2	3	4	5	6	7	8	9	10

I Cover the multiplication square but use it to check your answers **after** copying and completing these:

a $35 \div 7 = \square$ f $45 \div 5 = \square$

b $36 \div 4 = \square$ g $27 \div 3 = \square$

c $18 \div 2 = \square$ h $32 \div 8 = \square$

d $27 \div 9 = \square$ i $54 \div 6 = \square$

e $56 \div 8 = \square$ j $72 \div 8 = \square$

2 a

$\div 6$	6	42	30	18	48	60	54	36

c

$\div 8$	40	80	32	16	64	48	24	56

b

$\div 7$	14	21	7	63	49	42	70	56

d

$\div 9$	18	81	27	72	36	63	45	54

Here is another way to set out division:
"36 divided by 4 is $\square$"
or "How many sets of 4 are contained in 36?"

$$4\overline{)36}$$

The answer goes above the number you are dividing.

3 Copy and complete:

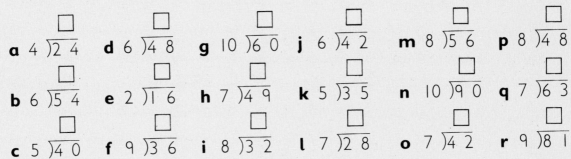

a $4\overline{)24}$ d $6\overline{)48}$ g $10\overline{)60}$ j $6\overline{)42}$ m $8\overline{)56}$ p $8\overline{)48}$

b $6\overline{)54}$ e $2\overline{)16}$ h $7\overline{)49}$ k $5\overline{)35}$ n $10\overline{)90}$ q $7\overline{)63}$

c $5\overline{)40}$ f $9\overline{)36}$ i $8\overline{)32}$ l $7\overline{)28}$ o $7\overline{)42}$ r $9\overline{)81}$

Division with remainders

Put 17 counters into rows of 5.

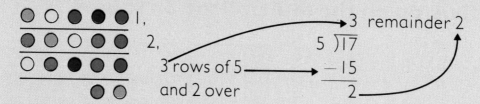

3 rows of 5 ───→ and 2 over

3 remainder 2

5)17
 −15
   2

$17 \div 5 = 3$, remainder 2.

On a number line $17 \div 5$ is shown like this.

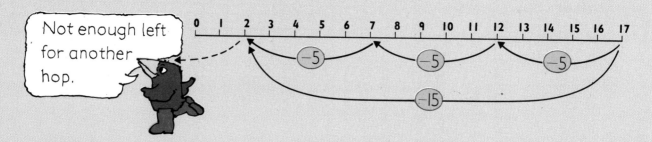

Not enough left for another hop.

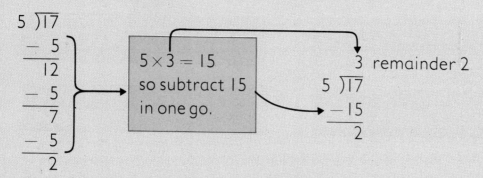

5)17
 − 5
  12
 − 5
   7
 − 5
   2

5 × 3 = 15
so subtract 15
in one go.

3 remainder 2

5)17
 −15
   2

Here are some more examples.

② remainder ④
5)14
 −10 (2 lots of 5)
   ④

③ remainder ②
6)20
 −18 (3 lots of 6)
   ②

④ remainder ③
6)27
 −24
   ③

I Copy and complete. (Use counters or a number line.)

a ☐ rem △
5)1 9
 −1 5
    4

b ☐ rem △
6)2 9
 −2 4
    5

c ☐ rem △
7)3 8
 −3 5
   △

d ☐ rem △
3)3 1
 −☐
  △

e ☐ rem △
8)4 7
 −☐
  △

1 Set these out the same way. (They all have remainders.)
Remember to leave space at the top for the answer.

a 5)22   **c** 10)37   **e** 7)45   **g** 9)75   **i** 9)89

b 6)34   **d** 9)44   **f** 3)29   **h** 4)39   **j** 8)67

2 Try these. (Some have remainders; some do not.)

a 2)19   **c** 5)36   **e** 8)57   **g** 10)57   **i** 9)63

b 2)18   **d** 6)36   **f** 9)64   **h** 7)50   **j** 8)64

3 **a** 34 eggs are packed into boxes, 6 in a box.
How many full boxes will there be?
How many eggs left over?

b To make a square, 4 triangles like this ▽ are fitted together ⊠
How many squares can be made from 39 triangles?
How many triangles will be left over?

c There are 7 players in a netball team.
How many teams can be formed from 32 players?
How many reserves will there be?

d You are given 60p to buy apples at 8p each.
How many can you buy and how much change will you have?

e How many pieces of ribbon 9 centimetres long can be cut
from a length 78 centimetres?
How much ribbon will be left?

f I gave 50p for 6 bags of crisps and got 2p change?
How much did each bag cost?

4 Copy and complete these "computer tapes".

÷9	10	20	30	40	50	60	70	80	90
	1 r 1								10 r 0

÷8	10	20	30	40	50	60	70	80	90
	1 r 2			5 r 0					11 r 2

Make up some more of your own. Look for patterns.

Chapter 17: Fractions

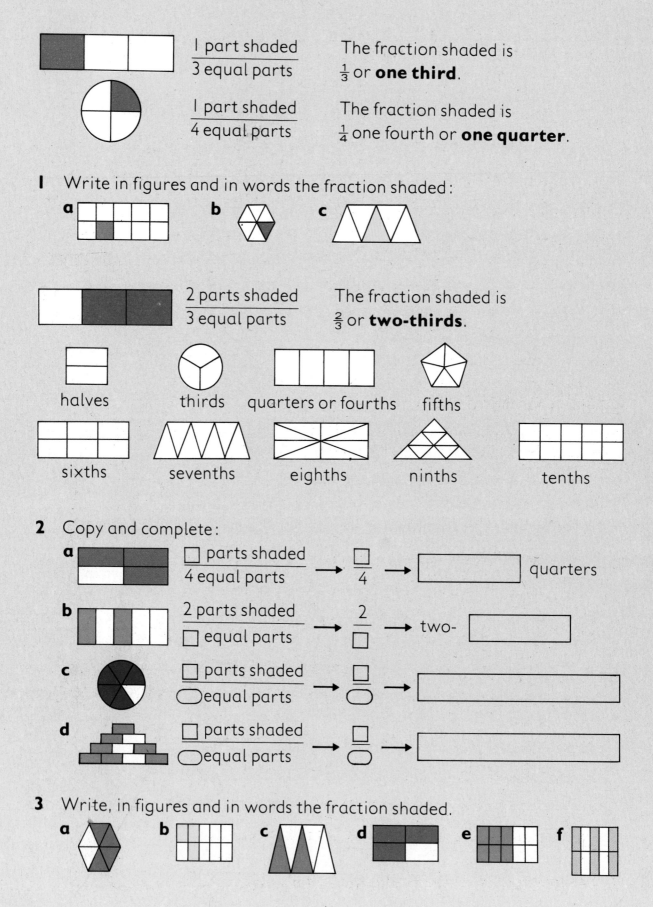

1 part shaded / 3 equal parts — The fraction shaded is $\frac{1}{3}$ or **one third**.

1 part shaded / 4 equal parts — The fraction shaded is $\frac{1}{4}$ one fourth or **one quarter**.

1 Write in figures and in words the fraction shaded :

   a   **b**   **c**

2 parts shaded / 3 equal parts — The fraction shaded is $\frac{2}{3}$ or **two-thirds**.

halves   thirds   quarters or fourths   fifths

sixths   sevenths   eighths   ninths   tenths

2 Copy and complete :

a ☐ parts shaded / 4 equal parts → $\frac{\square}{4}$ → ☐ quarters

b 2 parts shaded / ☐ equal parts → $\frac{2}{\square}$ → two- ☐

c ☐ parts shaded / ◯ equal parts → $\frac{\square}{\bigcirc}$ → ☐

d ☐ parts shaded / ◯ equal parts → $\frac{\square}{\bigcirc}$ → ☐

3 Write, in figures and in words the fraction shaded.

  a   **b**   **c**   **d**   **e**   **f**

In this set of 8 circles 5 are shaded.

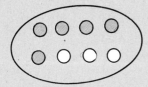

$\dfrac{5 \text{ shaded}}{8 \text{ in the whole set}} \rightarrow \frac{5}{8} \rightarrow$ five-eighths shaded

1 Write, in figures and in words, the fraction shaded.

a 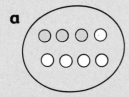   c 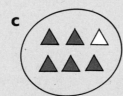   e 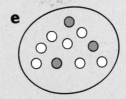   g

b 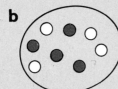   d 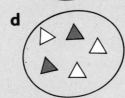   f 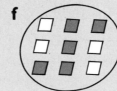   h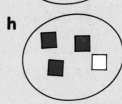

Fraction families

In each of these squares, the same fraction is shaded.

$\frac{1}{2}$  $\frac{2}{4}$ 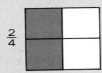 $\frac{3}{6}$ 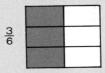 $\frac{4}{8}$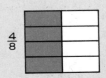

$\frac{1}{2}$, $\frac{2}{4}$, $\frac{3}{6}$, $\frac{4}{8}$ are different names for the same fraction.
They all belong to the "family of $\frac{1}{2}$".

2 Copy and complete: $\frac{1}{2} = \frac{2}{4} = \frac{3}{6} = \frac{4}{8} = \frac{5}{\square} = \frac{\triangle}{12} = \frac{10}{\square} = \frac{100}{\bigcirc}$

3 These diagrams show some of the "family of $\frac{1}{3}$".

Copy and complete:

$\frac{1}{3} = \frac{\square}{6} = \frac{3}{\triangle} = \frac{\bigcirc}{12}$

4 Write four more fractions in the "family of $\frac{1}{3}$".

5 Make a list of six fractions in the "family of $\frac{1}{5}$".

1 The diagrams show $\frac{3}{4} = \frac{6}{8} = \frac{12}{16}$.

Write four more fractions in
the "family of $\frac{3}{4}$".

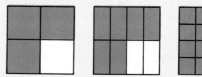

2 **a** On squared paper, draw diagrams to show that $\frac{2}{3} = \frac{4}{6} = \frac{8}{12}$
Write four more fractions in the "family of $\frac{2}{3}$".
b Do the same for $\frac{1}{5} = \frac{2}{10} = \frac{3}{15}$.

"The family of one"

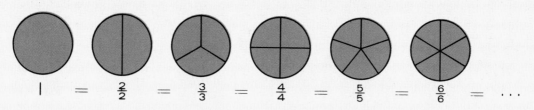

$$1 = \frac{2}{2} = \frac{3}{3} = \frac{4}{4} = \frac{5}{5} = \frac{6}{6} = \cdots$$

3 **a** Write ten more fractions in the "family of one".
b How many fractions are there in the "family of one"?

The fraction chart

4 Use strips of coloured paper or
card to make a fraction chart
like this.
The chart shows:
$\frac{1}{2} = \frac{2}{4} = \frac{4}{8} = \frac{3}{6} = \frac{5}{10}$

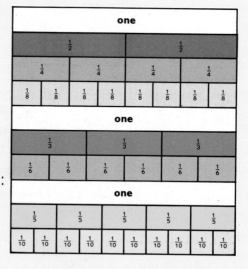

5 Use the chart to help you complete:

a $\frac{2}{3} = \frac{\square}{6}$ **c** $\frac{3}{4} = \frac{6}{\square}$ **e** $\frac{6}{10} = \frac{3}{\square}$

b $\frac{2}{5} = \frac{\square}{10}$ **d** $\frac{4}{8} = \frac{\square}{4}$ **f** $\frac{4}{\square} = \frac{8}{10}$

6 The chart also shows: $\frac{1}{2} > \frac{1}{4}$, $\frac{1}{3} < \frac{3}{8}$, $\frac{5}{6} > \frac{5}{8}$
Copy and complete by putting > (more than) or < (less than) between
these fractions.

a $\frac{1}{2} \square \frac{1}{4}$ **c** $\frac{3}{8} \square \frac{1}{2}$ **e** $\frac{7}{8} \square \frac{2}{3}$ **g** $\frac{3}{5} \square \frac{3}{4}$ **i** $\frac{1}{2} \square \frac{1}{3} \square \frac{1}{4}$

b $\frac{1}{6} \square \frac{1}{3}$ **d** $\frac{4}{5} \square \frac{2}{3}$ **f** $\frac{1}{2} \square \frac{2}{5}$ **h** $\frac{9}{10} \square \frac{7}{8}$ **j** $\frac{3}{10} \square \frac{3}{8} \square \frac{3}{5}$

"Fraction families" from the multiplication square

The multiplication square starts at the top left hand corner with 1×1. It goes up to 10×10 in the bottom right-hand corner. Cover up most of the square but leave the top two rows showing.

1	2	3	4	5	6	7	8	9	10
2	4	6	8	10	12	14	16	18	20
3	6	9	12	15	18	21	24	27	30
4	8	12	16	20	24	28	32	36	40
5	10	15	20	25	30	35	40	45	50
6	12	18	24	30	36	42	48	54	60
7	14	21	28	35	42	49	56	63	70
8	16	24	32	40	48	56	64	72	80
9	18	27	36	45	54	63	72	81	90
10	20	30	40	50	60	70	80	90	100

1	2	3	4	5	6	7	8	9	10
2	4	6	8	10	12	14	16	18	20

From this you can list some of the members of the "family of $\frac{1}{2}$".

$\frac{1}{2} = \frac{2}{4} = \frac{3}{6} = \frac{4}{8}$ etc.

But 2 and 4 also appear in the first column of the square.

By using strips of paper we can find more members of the "family of $\frac{1}{2}$".

2	4	6	8	10	12	14	16	18	20

4	8	12	16	20	24	28	32	36	40

$\frac{2}{4} = \frac{4}{8} = \frac{6}{12} = \frac{10}{20} = \underbrace{\frac{12}{24} = \frac{14}{28} = \frac{16}{32} = \frac{18}{36} = \frac{20}{40}}_{\text{new members}}$

Even more members of the "family of $\frac{1}{2}$" can be found by going along the 3 row and the 6 row:

3	6	9	12	15	18	21	24	27	30

6	12	18	24	30	36	42	48	54	60

$\frac{3}{6} = \frac{6}{12} = \frac{9}{18} = \frac{12}{24} = \frac{15}{30} = \frac{18}{36} = \frac{21}{42}$

1 See how many more of the "family of $\frac{1}{2}$", that is fractions equal to $\frac{1}{2}$, you can find,

    a looking along the 4 row and the 8 row.

    b looking along the 5 row and the 10 row.

2 Use the multiplication square to find as many members as you can in each of these families:

    a $\frac{1}{3}$ (Use rows 1 and 3, rows 2 and 6, rows 3 and 9)

    b $\frac{3}{4}$ (rows 3 and 4, rows 6 and 8)   **d** $\frac{2}{5}$ **f** $\frac{4}{5}$

    c $\frac{1}{5}$ (rows 1 and 5, rows 2 and 10)   **e** $\frac{3}{5}$ **g** $\frac{2}{3}$

This line, 12cm long, is divided into 3 equal parts.

$\frac{1}{3}$ of 12cm = 4cm $\frac{2}{3}$ of 12cm = 8cm

1 Draw a line 15cm long. Divide it into 5 equal parts.

a $\frac{1}{5}$ of 15cm is ☐cm   **b** $\frac{2}{5}$ of 15cm is ☐cm   **c** $\frac{4}{5}$ of 15cm is ☐cm

2 There are 27 children in a class and $\frac{1}{3}$ of them are boys.

a How many boys are there in the class?
b What fraction of the class are girls?
c How many girls are there in the class?

3 Draw this flag and colour $\frac{1}{3}$ of the squares blue, $\frac{1}{4}$ of the squares red and leave the rest white.

a How many squares of each colour are there?
b What fraction of the flag is white?

4 Altogether the children in a class have 20 pets.
$\frac{1}{5}$ are cats, $\frac{2}{5}$ are dogs, $\frac{1}{10}$ are fish and $\frac{3}{10}$ rabbits.
How many of each animal are there?

Adding fractions to make 1

5 One whole divided into 8 equal parts

1 part black
2 parts white
5 parts shaded

Fraction sentence:
$\frac{1}{8}+\frac{2}{8}+\frac{5}{8}=\frac{8}{8}=1$

Write the fraction sentences for these:

a   **c**   **e**   **g**   **i**

b   **d**   **f**   **h**   **j**
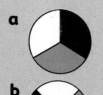

Chapter 18: Time

From one time to another

Look at the two clock faces:
By counting on, you can work out
that from 9.05 to 9.27 is
22 minutes.

Start counting here

1 Copy and complete the sentences under these clocks.

a

From ☐ to ☐
is ☐ minutes.

c

From ☐ to ☐
is ☐ minutes.

b

From ☐ to ☐
is ☐ minutes.

d

From ☐ to ☐
is ☐ hours ☐ minutes.

2 a Sue should be at school by quarter past nine but she arrived at 9.32.
How many minutes late was she?

b The first half of a match started at 3.04 and lasted 45 minutes. What
time did the half-time whistle go?

c Peter put his cake into the oven at 6 minutes to 10.
When should he take it out if the baking time is 35 minutes?

d When Anne started reading, her watch showed | 9:32 | ; when
she finished, it said | 10:45 | . For how long was she reading?

Slow and fast

A clock does not always show the correct time. It may run too slowly and get behind the real time. For example, if the real time is 8.15 and the clock shows 8.10, you say, "It is 5 minutes slow" or "It has lost 5 minutes".

5 minutes **slow**

Real time: 8.15

Some clocks go too fast and get ahead of the real time. This clock is a quarter of an hour fast.
     It has gained a quarter of an hour.

15 minutes **fast**

1 If the real time is 5.49, write down how fast each of these clocks is:

2 Write down how many minutes slow each of the clocks is if the real time is 7.12.

3 Write down the correct time which should be shown by each of these digital watches.

   a `10:03`   **b** `12:38`   **c** `11:27`   **d** `10:13`

Watch **a** is 10 mins fast.   Watch **b** is 8 mins slow.   Watch **c** has lost 14 mins.   Watch **d** has gained 6 mins.

4 The clock in Gary's house gains 1 minute every day.
     He puts it right at mid-day on Monday.
     What time will it show at mid-day on the following Saturday?

5 The clock in Lucy's house loses half a minute a day.
     How many minutes will it lose in the month of April?

6 What are two ways of finding out if your clock is showing the right time?

7 Which clock shows exactly the correct time twice every day?

a.m. and p.m.

There are 24 hours in the day.
The hour hand goes round the clock twice
in a day.

> I'll meet you at
> 8 o'clock on Saturday.

> In the morning
> or the evening?

So that you can tell the difference between 8 in the morning
and 8 in the evening, each day is split into two halves.
Times from midnight to mid-day are called **a.m.**
Times after mid-day up to the next midnight are called **p.m.**

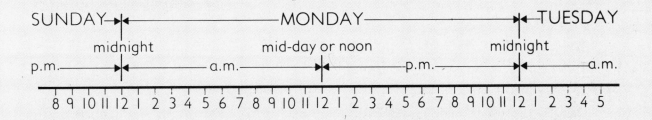

"a.m." and "p.m." are short for Latin words –
ante meridiem ("before noon") and **post meridiem** ("after noon").

I   Find out what the words **antechamber**, **antenatal**,
    postmortem, and **postscript** mean.

2   Use the diagram above like a "time ruler" to find
    the number of hours between:
    a 10 a.m. on Monday and 8 p.m. on Monday
    b 4 p.m. on Monday and 1 a.m. on Tuesday
    c 11 p.m. on Sunday and noon on Monday
    d 10 p.m. on Sunday and 2 a.m. on Tuesday

3   Write these times in figures with either a.m. or p.m.
    a Twenty past eight in the morning   **d** Five minutes to midnight
    b Ten to eight in the evening   **e** One minute past noon
    c Half past two in the afternoon   **f** Twelve minutes past midnight

4   How many hours and minutes are there from 8.30 a.m. to:
    a 11.45 a.m.   **b** 1.40 p.m.   **c** 12.05 p.m.   **d** 6.20 p.m. on the same day?

The calendar

Here is a page from a calendar for
the month of October, 1981.

October 1981						
Sun	Mon	Tues	Wed	Thur	Fri	Sat
				1	2	3
4	5	6	7	8	9	10
11	12	13	14	15	16	17
18	19	20	21	22	23	24
25	26	27	28	29	30	31

1　**a** On which days of the week are
　　　the first and last days of the month?
　　b How many days are there in the month?
　　c How many school days are there in
　　　the month (if there are no extra holidays)?
　　d On which day of the week is the
　　　2nd November?

2　Here are the months of the year in a jumbled order:
　　January, August, May, September, February, December, October,
　　March, June, April, July, November.

　　a Write them down in the right order.
　　b Four of these months have 30 days in them.
　　　Write their names down.
　　c Which month usually has 28 days?
　　　How many does it sometimes have? When does this happen?

3　Ann's 9th birthday is on 30th September 1981.
　　Mary's 9th birthday is on 3rd November 1981.
　　Who is older, and by how many days?

4　Mary writes the date when she was born like this: 3.11.72.

　　a What does the 3 stand for? What does the 11 stand for?
　　　What is the 72 short for?
　　b Can you write this date in two other ways?
　　c How old will she be on her birthday in 1987?

5　Write the dates when these events happen.

　　a Christmas Day　　　**c** St. Valentine's Day　　**e** April Fool's Day
　　b New Year's Day　　　**d** St. Swithen's Day　　　**f** Chrismas Eve

1 Look at the fourth column of the calendar (under Wed.).
    a Where have you seen these numbers before?
    b Why do they happen here?

2 How many days are there in: **a** 3 weeks?   **b** 5 weeks?

3 How many weeks are there in: **a** 63 days?   **b** 42 days?

4 Here is a page from a calendar, but the bottom has been torn off:

JANUARY 1982						
Sun	Mon	Tues	Wed	Thur	Fri	Sat
					1	2

    a Draw the full calendar page for January in your book and fill in all the missing days.
    b What day of the week will the 51st day of the year be?
    c What day of the week will 17th February fall on?
    d What day of the week will 1st March fall on?

Leap years

Look at these pages from calendars for 1983 and 1984.

There is an extra day in 1984 because 1984 is a **leap year**.

A leap year has 366 days instead of 365.

FEBRUARY 1983						
S	M	T	W	T	F	S
		1	2	3	4	5
6	7	8	9	10	11	12
13	14	15	16	17	18	19
20	21	22	23	24	25	26
27	28					

FEBRUARY 1984						
S	M	T	W	T	F	S
		1	2	3	4	
5	6	7	8	9	10	11
12	13	14	15	16	17	18
19	20	21	22	23	24	25
26	27	28	29			

The extra day is given to February because it is the shortest month.

5 Here are some more leap years: 1960, 1964, 1968, 1972, 1976, 1980.
    a What is the pattern for leap years?
    b Write a list of the next 5 leap years beginning with 1984.
    c Find out why we have leap years.
    d Do you know anyone whose birthday is on February 29th? What do they do about their birthdays on non-leap years?

Chapter 19: Multiplication 2

Multiplying in parts

The soldier has
14 buttons on his coat.
7 in each column:
$7 \times 2 = 14$

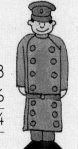

Now he has his belt on.
Above the belt: $4 \times 2 = 8$
Below the belt: $3 \times 2 = 6$
Altogether: $\overline{14}$

Instead of multiplying 7×2:   Separate into parts: $(4+3) \times 2$ Multiply each part on its own: Add the parts together again.

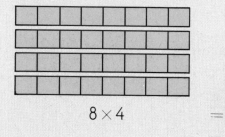

$4 \times 2 = 8$

$3 \times 2 = 6$

$\Big\}$ 14

This time 8×4 is separated into parts.

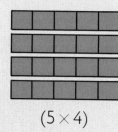   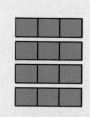

8×4 $=$ (5×4) $+$ (3×4)
$=$ 20 $+$ 12 $= 32$

I Use cubes or counters for these.

a $5 \times 4 = (3 \times 4) + (2 \times 4)$
$= 12 + \bigcirc = \square$

e $9 \times 5 = (5 \times 5) + (\square \times 5)$
$= 25 + \bigcirc = \square$

b $9 \times 4 = (6 \times 4) + (3 \times 4)$
$= \bigcirc + 12 = \square$

f $8 \times 7 = (6 \times 7) + (\square \times 7)$
$= 42 + \bigcirc = \square$

c $9 \times 4 = (7 \times 4) + (2 \times 4)$
$= \bigcirc + 8 = \square$

g $8 \times 7 = (\square \times 7) + (3 \times 7)$
$= \bigcirc + 21 = \square$

d $9 \times 5 = (6 \times 5) + (3 \times 5)$
$= \bigcirc + 15 = \square$

h $7 \times 6 = (4 \times 6) + (\square \times 6)$
$= 24 + \bigcirc = \square$

Multiplying tens and unit by units

Splitting a number into parts and multiplying each part separately is useful for larger numbers.

The diagram shows 13×4

13×4 is set out like this:

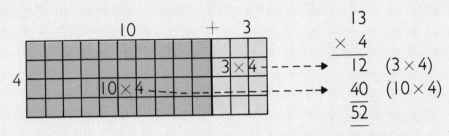

```
  13
×  4
────
  12   (3 × 4)
  40   (10 × 4)
────
  52
```

I Set out the multiplications in the same way for these:

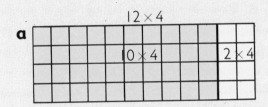

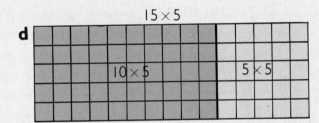

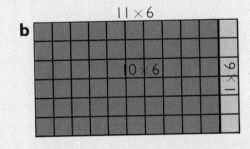

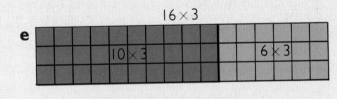

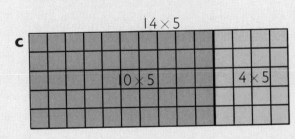

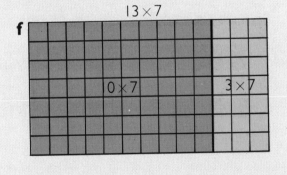

This diagram shows 24×3:

It is set out like this:

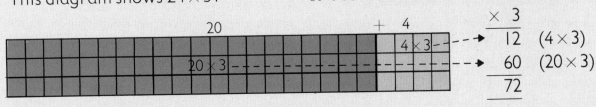

```
  24
×  3
────
  12   (4 × 3)
  60   (20 × 3)
────
  72
```

1 Set these out the same way:

a	13×5	**e**	14×7	**i**	22×8	**m**	31×6
b	17×3	**f**	13×9	**j**	29×5	**n**	37×3
c	19×2	**g**	21×4	**k**	27×6	**o**	42×4
d	16×7	**h**	26×3	**l**	23×7	**p**	53×5

2 **a** How many eggs are there altogether in 17 boxes with 6 eggs in each box?

   b Seats for a concert are set out in 8 rows with 14 in a row. How many seats are there?

   c What is the product of 13 and 9?

   d How much will it cost to take 7 children for a bus ride if the fare is 16 pence each?

   e If a crayon weighs 26 grams, what do 4 crayons weigh?

   f Find the answer to 12+12+12+12+12+12 by multiplication.

   g A medicine spoon holds 5 millilitres. How much medicine have you had after taking 27 spoonfuls?

   h A gramophone record does 33 complete turns every minute. How many times does it turn in 4 minutes?

   i The area of a stamp is 13 square centimetres. What area will be covered by 8 of these stamps?

   j A racing car travels 38 metres in a second. How far does it go in 6 seconds?

3 Copy and complete, then look for patterns:

factor	16	32	64	14	28	21	42	12	36	18	12
factor	8	4	2	6	3	4	2	7	2	4	6
product											

4

21	14	19
16	18	20
17	22	15

Multiply each number in this magic square by 2. Check that your new square is "magic" by adding rows, columns and diagonals.
Make up some more magic squares by multiplying by 3, 4, 5 etc.

Chapter 20: Money 2

More writing in pounds and pence

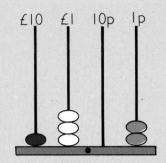

The abacus records £13 and 2 pence.
You write £13·02.
You must show that one of
the abacus columns is empty
by putting a zero in that place.
Remember the zero tells you there were no ten pence.

1 Draw an abacus to record each of the following amounts.
   a £34·06   **b** £5·04   **c** £30·60   **d** £38·05   **e** £20·90   **f** £34·02

Because there are one hundred pence in one pound.
you can write either £1·00 or 100p.
One pound and thirty-five pence can be written as £1·35 or 135p.

2 Write these amounts in two ways.
   First write them in pounds then in pence.
   a Five pounds and forty-nine pence
   b Fifteen pounds and sixty-eight pence
   c Sixteen pounds and twenty-three pence

3 Write these amounts in pounds: **a** 456p   **b** 372p   **c** 914p   **d** 802p

4 Write these amounts in pence: **a** £5·71   **b** £3·66   **c** £9·92   **d** £7·08

Listing amounts of money

5 Write these amounts in pounds.
   Put them in columns, keeping the decimal points under each other,
   like this:

                                    £
   £1·23, 46p, £4·00, £0·06   1·23   **a** £2·35, 27p, £5, 6p
                              0·46   **b** £2·04, 81p, £10, 1p
                              4·00   **c** 1p, £4·50, 75p, 190p
                              0·06   **d** £1, 1p, 234p, £6·32

1 Write these amounts in pence.
Put them in columns like this:

87p, 8p, £1·34, 105p

p
87
8
134
105

a 56p, £2·16, 63p, 5p
b 103p, £1·63, 53p, 5p
c £2, 99p, 14p, 9p
d 10p, 20p, £2·56, 2p

2 In a gift shop these items are on sale.

 book £1·05   teddybear £3·99    tennis racket £4   crayons 85p

 camera £4·50    draughts £1·25   pencil case 50p

a Write a list of the gifts which have prices less than £1.
b Write a list of the gifts which cost more than £1 but less than £2.
c List the gifts which cost more than £2.
d Write a list of the gifts with their prices in order, starting from the cheapest.
e If 10p is taken off each of the prices, make a list of the gifts showing their new prices.
f If 20p is added to each of the prices shown in the picture make a list of the gifts with their new prices.

Other ways of saying prices

 Bargain price £1·68

When we go shopping we sometimes call this amount "one pound, sixty-eight" or "one sixty-eight".

We mean one pound and sixty-eight pence, which is written as £1·68.

3 Here are some for you to do. Record these amounts in figures.
a One pound forty-five
b Three pounds sixty-one
c Five ninety-nine
d Two pounds four pence
e Twelve fifty
f One pound ten pence
g Ten pounds
h Seven pounds seventy
i One penny less than £3

Addition of money

1   Copy and add these amounts. Remember – decimal points should always be beneath each other.

a £	b £	c £	d £	e £	f £
3·32	3·36	5·05	5·19	7·41	6·89
+1·53	+2·12	+2·12	+2·34	+3·48	+2·34
4·14	3·41	1·47	3·57	2·65	1·35

g £5·83+£2·50+£2·33   h £3·32+£4·93+£4·47

2   a I spent £1·05 on a book, £4·75 on a record and 75p on
        a packet of crayons. How much did I spend altogether?
    b Jill has £5 for her birthday. She would like to buy a scrap book
        for £1·25, a pair of scissors for £2·56 and some new paints for £1·05.
        Can she afford to buy them all?

Finding the change by counting on

3   Find the change by counting on in these examples. Use your coins if you
    need them. Copy and complete the table.

	price	amount given to shopkeeper	change
a	65p	£1·00	
b	£0·42	£1·00	
c	£1·24	£2·00	
d	£1·51	£2·00	

	price	amount given to shopkeeper	change
e	£2·21	£3·00	
f	£0·19	£1·00	
g	£3·64	£4·00	
h	£1·55	£2·00	

Subtraction of money

1   Copy and complete the following subtractions. Remember – the decimal points should always be beneath one another.

a £	**b** £	**c** £	**d** £	**e** £	**f** £
8·76	7·43	5·37	6·17	7·60	8·00
−2·54	−2·27	−3·48	−3·38	−2·49	−4·32

Multiplication of money

The cost of 4kg of potatoes at 15p per kg can be found by addition, but multiplying is quicker.
4kg will cost:

 15p +   15p +   15p +   15p

$$
\begin{array}{r}
15p \\
\times\ 4 \\
\hline
20 \quad (5 \times 4) \\
40 \quad (10 \times 4) \\
\hline
60p
\end{array}
$$

Complete these:

2   **a** 6kg of potatoes at 14p per kg
    b 7 metres of cord at 13p per metre
    c 4 litres of beer at 24p per litre
    d 2kg of sweets at 23p per 500g
    e 5 metres of wire at 18p per metre
    f 4kg of cheese at 50p per $\frac{1}{2}$kg
    g Half a dozen eggs at 8p each
    h 8m² carpet at £12 per m²

Division of money

3   **a** 4 eggs cost 28p. What is the cost of 1 egg?
    b How many children can be given 5p each from 45p?
    c Share 63p equally between 7 children.
    d If 8 metres of ribbon cost 56p, find the cost of one metre.
    e How many pence in $\frac{1}{5}$ of a pound?

Chapter 21: Volume and Capacity 2

Using capacity measures

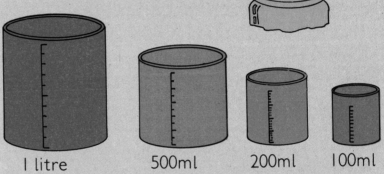

If you want to put 75ml of water into a jar, here are two ways to measure the right amount.

The first way is to fill the 50ml, 20ml and 5ml containers and empty them all into the jar.

The other way is to use a measure bigger than 75ml with a scale of ml marked down the side.

These measures come in different sizes.

1 litre   500ml   200ml   100ml

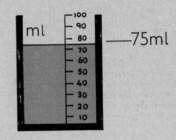

To measure 75ml you take the 100ml measure and fill it till the water reaches the 75ml mark.

Do you know why the 100ml measure has been used and not one of the bigger ones?

1 Use the first way (with smaller measures) to measure out the following amounts of water. Record in your book the containers you have used each time.

a 25ml	**c** 85ml	**e** 140ml	**g** 350ml	**i** 885ml
b 60ml	**d** 110ml	**f** 165ml	**h** 720ml	**j** 915ml

2 Use the second way (with a marked measure) to measure out the following amounts of water. Record in your book the smallest container which will hold each amount.

a 35ml	**c** 95ml	**e** 250ml	**g** 490ml	**i** 750ml
b 60ml	**d** 120ml	**f** 350ml	**h** 625ml	**j** 1000ml

Millilitres as fractions of a litre

Look at this set
of measures.
There is a new one –
250ml.

1 litre   500ml   250ml   200ml   100ml   50ml

1 a How many times can the 250ml container be filled from
   the 1 litre container? (Try to work this out without
   using real containers.)
   b What fraction is 250ml of 1 litre?
   c Which container holds $\frac{1}{2}$ litre?
   d If the 200ml container is filled twice from the $\frac{1}{2}$ litre container, how
   many ml of water would be left in the larger container?
   e How many times must the 50ml container be filled to make $\frac{1}{4}$ litre?
   f How many ml are there in $\frac{3}{4}$ litre?

2 Copy and complete
   a $\frac{1}{2}$ litre + $\square$ml = 1 litre   c $\square$ml + 250ml = $\frac{3}{4}$ litre
   b 750ml + $\square$ml = 1 litre   d 150ml + $\square$ml = $\frac{1}{4}$ litre

Here is a graph showing the capacities
of some containers.

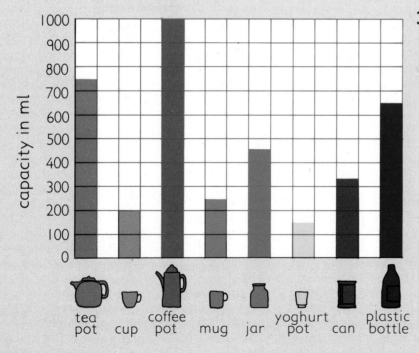

3 Look at the graph
  carefully and answer
  these questions.
  a How much does
    the cup hold?
  b What is the capacity
    of the jar?
  c Which holds $\frac{3}{4}$
    litre?
  d Could you fill 2
    cups from the can?
  e How many more
    millilitres does a mug
    hold than a cup?

The marks on 1 litre measures

These 1 litre measures have sides marked in ml.
(Remember, there are 1000ml in 1 litre.)
They contain different amounts of water.

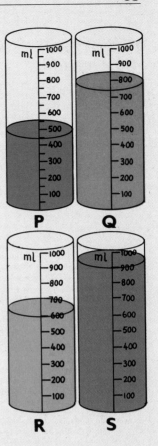

1 a How many ml of water are there in measure **P**?
b How many ml of water are there in measure **Q**?
c How many more ml are needed to fill measure **Q**?
d Which of the two measures together have enough
water in them to make 1½ litres?
e By how many ml is the water in **R** less than 1 litre?
f How many 150ml glasses can be filled from **S**?
g How much more water is shown in **S** than in **R**?

More than a litre

In this bottle is 1 litre and 650 millilitres of fruit juice.
To record this you could write: 1 litre and 650ml.
Another way is to write litres
and millilitres in separate columns.
An even shorter way is to separate litres and
millilitres with a **decimal point**.

	litres	ml	
1 litre and 650ml	1	650	1·650 litres

2 Copy and complete this table.

		litres	ml	litres
a	2 litres and 450ml	2	450	2·450
b	3 litres and 250ml	☐	☐	☐
c	5 litres and 180ml	☐	☐	☐
d	☐ litres ☐ml	☐	☐	4·550
e	☐ litres and ☐ml	☐	☐	3·820

Look carefully at the liquid in these measuring jars:

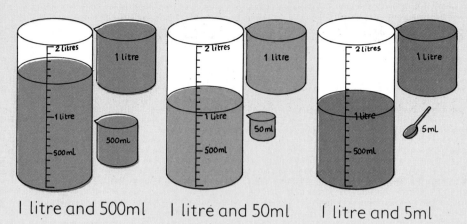

I litre and 500ml   I litre and 50ml   I litre and 5ml

How do we write down these capacities?

litres	ml
I litre and 500ml	I	5 0 0	1·500 litres
I litre and 50ml	I	5 0	1·050 litres
I litre and 5ml	I	5	1·005 litres

1·050 litres ← This shows that there are **no** hundreds of millilitres. The number of millilitres is **less than 100**.

1·005 litres ← These show that there are **no** hundreds and **no** tens of millilitres. The number of millilitres is **less than 10**.

1 Copy and complete.

litres	ml	
2	700	= 2·700 litres
☐	☐	= ☐ litres
☐	☐	= ☐ litres
☐	☐	= ☐ litres
☐	☐	= ☐ litres
☐	☐	= ☐ litres
☐	☐	= ☐ litres

a 2 litres and 700ml
b 2 litres and 70ml
c 2 litres and 7ml
d 3 litres and 255ml
e I litre and 75ml
f 950ml
g 95ml

2 Use the I litre measure and any smaller measures you need to find the capacity of some larger containers. Estimate the capacity first; pour I litre of water if it helps you to estimate.

Record like this:

container	estimate litres	measurement litres
bucket	8·500	9·730

Chapter 22: Division 2

Division – larger numbers

For 91 ÷ 7, we could put out 91 counters in rows of 7
and count the rows. This would take a long time.

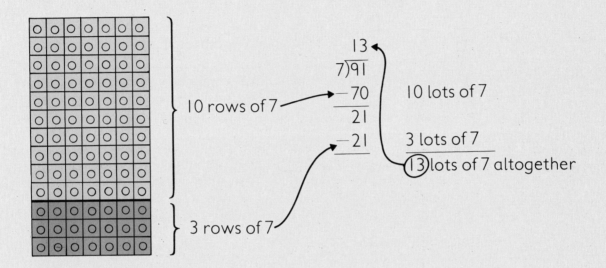

Because 7 × 10 = 70 and 70 < 91 we take away 10 lots of 7 first.
This leaves a smaller number to split into lots of 7.

I Here are some more diagrams. Look carefully at each one
then copy and complete the written part.

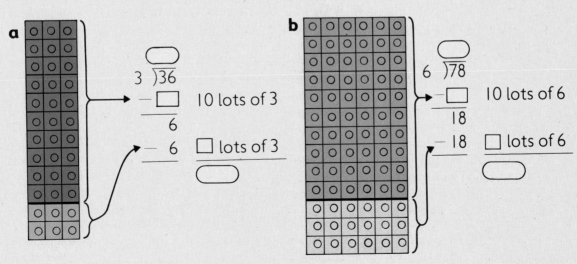

I Copy and complete

a 4)6 4 ⬭
 −□ | I 0 lots of 4
 ‾‾‾
 2 4
 −2 4 | □ lots of 4
 ‾‾‾ | ⬭ lots of 4

c 5)8 5 ⬭
 □ | I 0 lots of 5
 ‾‾‾
 3 5
 −3 5 | □ lots of 5
 ‾‾‾ | ⬭ lots of 5

e 6)9 6 ⬭
 −□ | I 0 lots of 6
 ‾‾‾
 3 6
 −3 6 | □ lots of 6
 ‾‾‾ | ⬭ lots of 6

b 8)9 6 ⬭
 −□ | I 0 lots of 8
 ‾‾‾
 I 6
 −I 6 | □ lots of 8
 ‾‾‾ | ⬭ lots of 8

d 7)9 8 ⬭
 −□ | I 0 lots of 7
 ‾‾‾
 2 8
 −□ | □ lots of 7
 ‾‾‾ | ⬭ lots of 7

f 4)7 6 ⬭
 −□ | I 0 lots of 4
 ‾‾‾
 3 6
 −□ | □ lots of 4
 ‾‾‾ | ⬭ lots of 4

2 a I 0 + □ = ⬭
 2)3 2
 −□ | I 0 (2)
 ‾‾‾
 I 2
 −□ | □ (2)
 ‾‾‾

d I 0 + □ = ⬭
 3)5 7
 −□ | I 0 (3)
 ‾‾‾
 2 7
 −□ | □ (3)
 ‾‾‾

g I 0 + □ = ⬭
 6)8 4
 −□ | I 0 (6)
 ‾‾‾
 2 4
 −□ | □ (6)
 ‾‾‾

b I 0 + □ = ⬭
 3)4 5
 −□ | I 0 (3)
 ‾‾‾
 I 5
 −□ | □ (3)
 ‾‾‾

e I 0 + □ = ⬭
 4)6 8
 −□ | I 0 (4)
 ‾‾‾
 2 8
 −□ | □ (4)
 ‾‾‾

h I 0 + □ = ⬭
 6)9 0
 −□ | I 0 (6)
 ‾‾‾
 3 0
 −□ | □ (6)
 ‾‾‾

c I 0 + □ = ⬭
 3)5 I
 −□ | I 0 (3)
 ‾‾‾
 2 I
 −□ | □ (3)
 ‾‾‾

f I 0 + □ = ⬭
 5)8 0
 −□ | I 0 (5)
 ‾‾‾
 3 0
 −□ | □ (5)
 ‾‾‾

i I 0 + □ = ⬭
 7)8 4
 −□ | I 0 (7)
 ‾‾‾
 I 4
 −□ | 2 (7)
 ‾‾‾

Division with remainders

1 Copy and complete

a
$$1\ 0+7 = 17$$
$$2\ )3\ 5$$
$$-\square$$
$$1\ 5$$
$$-1\ 4$$
$$1\ \text{remainder}$$

b
$$1\ 0+4 = 14$$
$$3\ )4\ 4$$
$$-\square$$
$$1\ 4$$
$$-1\ 2$$
$$\triangle\ \text{remainder}$$

c
$$1\ 0+\square = \bigcirc$$
$$4\ )6\ 3$$
$$-4\ 0$$
$$2\ 3$$
$$-\square$$
$$\triangle\ \text{remainder}$$

2 Set these out in the same way:

a $2\ )\overline{33}$ c $3\ )\overline{29}$ e $7\ )\overline{97}$ g $8\ )\overline{98}$ i $6\ )\overline{94}$

b $3\ )\overline{41}$ d $4\ )\overline{65}$ f $6\ )\overline{83}$ h $5\ )\overline{89}$ j $9\ )\overline{100}$

3 a To make a hexagon ⬡ six triangles like this △ are fitted together.
How many hexagons can be made from 89 triangles?
How many triangles are left?

b 75 pencils are put into boxes with 4 in each box.
How many full boxes will there be and how many pencils left over?

c How many days are there altogether in March, April and May?
How many full weeks is this?

d A medicine spoon holds 5 millilitres.
How many spoonfuls can you pour from a bottle holding
88 millilitres and how much is left in the bottle?

e How many books 4 centimetres wide can be placed side by side
on a shelf 50 centimetres long?

f In the dining hall, 6 children sit at each table.
If there are 89 children how many full tables
will there be?

g How many teams of 7 can be formed from 90 children?
How many will not be in a team?

Chapter 23: Weight 2

Scales with a dial

Many kinds of scales do not need weights.
A pointer points to a mark on a dial
to show the weight.
The letter weighs 100g.
These kitchen scales show that
the apples weigh 300g.

1 Record the weights shown on this dial
When the pointer is at **A**, **B**, **C** and **D**.

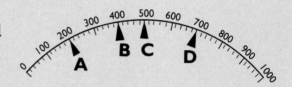

If the pointer stops between two figures you have
to work out what the marks stand for.

Pointer **E** is halfway between 200 and 300,
that is 250 grams.

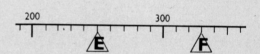

Each little mark stands for 10g.
Count on in 10's from 300 up to pointer **F**, that is 330 grams.

2 Copy and complete.
   a The weights on
      the dial are
      numbered every ☐ g.
   b The pointer marked
      letter ☐ is midway
      between 0 and 200g.
   c The small markings
      stand for ☐ g each.

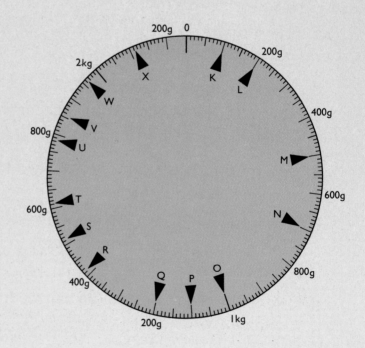

3 Record the weights shown
   by all the letters K to X.

Grams and kilograms

An object weighs I kg and 350g. You can write I kg and 350g.
A better way is to write kg and g in separate columns.
An even shorter way is to separate the kg and the g with a
decimal point.

	kg	g	
I kg and 350g	I	350	1·350kg

I Copy and complete this table.

kg g

a 3kg and 250g = ☐ ☐ = ☐

b I kg and 900g = ☐ ☐ = ☐

c 6kg and 630g = ☐ ☐ = ☐

d 10·700kg = ☐ ☐ = ☐

e 0·325kg = ☐ ☐ = ☐

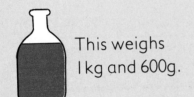

This weighs
I kg and 600g.

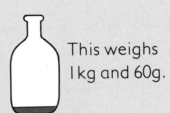

This weighs
I kg and 60g.

1·060 kg
↑ This shows that
there are NO hundreds
of grams. The number
of grams is *less than 100*.

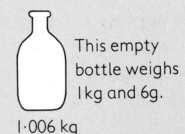

This empty
bottle weighs
I kg and 6g.

1·006 kg
↑↑ These show
that there are NO
hundreds and NO
tens of grams.
The number of
grams is *less than 10*.

kg g

I kg and 600g = 1 | 600 = 1·600kg
I kg and 60g = 1 | 60 = 1·060kg
I kg and   6g = 1 | 6 = 1·006kg

2 kg | g

a 3kg and 80g = ☐ ☐ = ☐ kg

b 3kg and 8g = ☐ ☐ = ☐ kg

c I kg and 90g = ☐ ☐ = ☐ kg

Weights on packets

Most food packets are marked with their weight in grams.
We always write grams or g for short.

1 Copy this list out on a piece of paper.
   Take the list home. Find as many of
   the items as you can.
   Write down the weight it says
   on each packet.

   Collect empty packets and labels from
   cans, and lists of things which show
   weights in kilograms or grams.

food packet	weight in g
packet of tea	
packet of soup	
can of fruit	
salad cream	
bottle of sauce	
packet of jelly	
can of meat	
packet of cereal	

Parts of a kilogram

2 Some kinds of cheese are sold
   in long blocks. Here are three
   1 kg slices taken from a block.

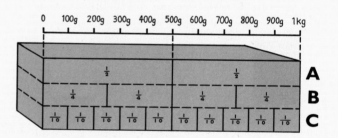

3 Copy and complete: (The picture will help you.)
   a Slice **A** is cut into two $\frac{1}{2}$ pieces. Each piece weighs☐ g.
   b Slice **B** is cut into four $\frac{1}{4}$ pieces. Each piece weighs☐ g.
   c Slice **C** is cut into ten $\frac{1}{10}$ pieces. Each piece weighs☐ g.
   d $\frac{1}{4}$kg =☐ g   e $\frac{3}{4}$kg =☐ g   f $\frac{3}{10}$kg =☐ g   g $\frac{7}{10}$kg =☐ g

Very heavy things

When weighing very heavy things
we use kilograms only.

4 List 10 other objects or animals
   heavier than 1 kg and estimate how heavy they are.

5 Make a list of the weights of four children in your class.

Chapter 24: Shape 2

1   Copy these shapes onto squared paper. Cut them out
    and fold them so that one part fits exactly on the other.
    The fold is an **axis of symmetry**.

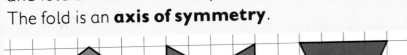

2   Copy these shapes onto squared paper and draw in
    their axes of symmetry.

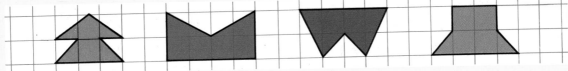

3   If you place a mirror along the dotted line in these half shapes
    you will see the complete picture. Copy and complete these:

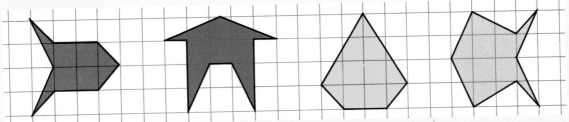

4   Some shapes have more than one axis of symmetry. Copy these onto
    squared paper. Cut them out. Fold them along as many axes of
    symmetry as you can find. The first has its axes marked for you.

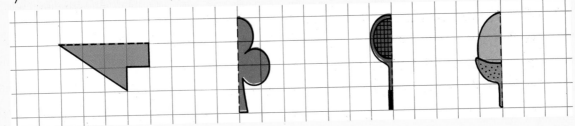

I Some of the capital letters of the alphabet have axes of symmetry.
Make a list of them marking the axes of symmetry.
Here are the first three.

2 Cut out a large square from a piece of paper.
Fold it into two equal parts along the axis
of symmetry shown in the diagram.
(How do you know the two parts are equal?)

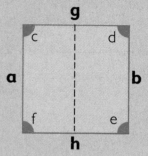

> Every time we fold a shape along an axis of symmetry we discover
> something about the shape because sides and angles which fit on
> each other are equal.

The fold shows that side **a** is the same length as side **b** and that
angle **c** is the same size as angle **d**. What other two angles are equal?

3 Unfold the cut-out shape and then fold it
along the axis of symmetry shown in this diagram.
Copy and complete the following sentences.

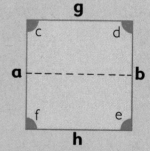

a Side **g** is the same length as side ☐.
b Angle **c** is the same size as angle ☐.
c Angle **e** is the same size as angle ☐.

4 Unfold the cut-out square and then fold it along
the axis of symmetry shown in this diagram.
Copy and complete the following.

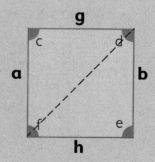

a Side **a** is the same length as side ☐.
b Side **g** is the same length as side ☐.
c Angle **c** is the same size as angle ☐.

1 Cut a large oblong from a piece of paper
and letter the sides and angles as in
the diagram.

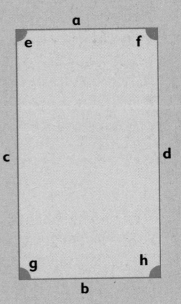

a Fold it along the horizontal axis of symmetry.

b Write a sentence about sides which are equal.

c Write two sentences about angles which
are the same size.

d Fold it along the vertical line of symmetry
and write three similar sentences.

e Fold the oblong along a diagonal (corner
to corner). Does this tell you anything
about the shape?

2 Copy this triangle onto a piece of squared paper
and cut it out.

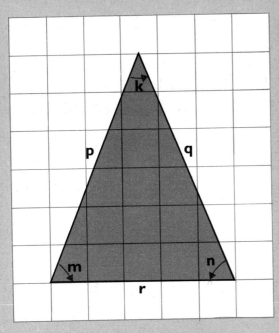

a Fold it along its axis of symmetry.

b Fold and complete one of
the following:

Side **p** is the same length as
side ☐

Angle **m** is the same size as
angle ☐

This triangle has a special name.

It is called an **isosceles triangle**.

The word isosceles comes from two
Greek words which mean equal legs.

We can see why from this drawing.

1 This shape is called an **equilateral triangle**.
Trace it onto a piece of paper and cut it out.

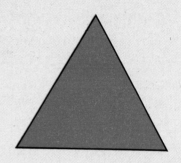

    a How many axes of symmetry are there?
    b What can you discover about its sides?
    c Write a sentence about the angles.

2 Copy these shapes onto squared paper.

Cut them out.

On each one write how many axes of symmetry you can discover
then mark with the same colour the sides which are equal.

Do the same for angles which are the same size.

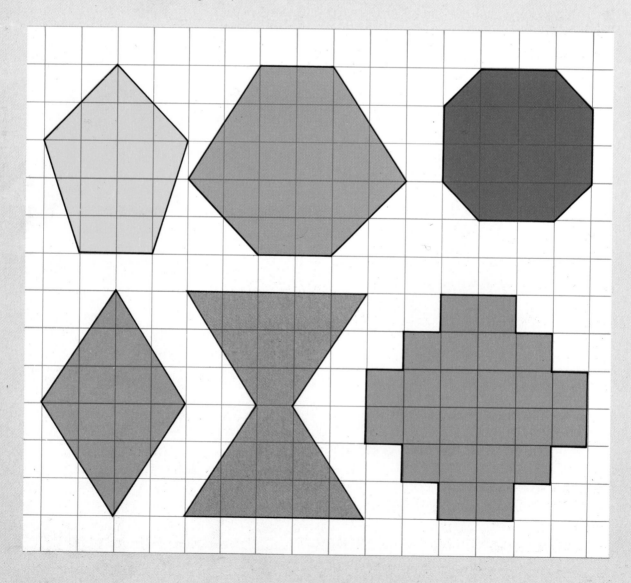